More First Perspectives on *At the Thresholds of Elysium*

"In this masterful 'book of lyrical illuminations' there is no safe place for anything to hide from Douglas Metcalf Gillette's poetics. He is a collector who puts before us everything from chickadees to dark matter, to his daughter, and time and things that shouldn't really matter, like corners and glimpses. His is a world that brightens gladly to reveal itself in words I had to look up in the dictionary; yes, in fact, even words can't hide from his wanton gaze. And no matter where we find ourselves there is God rising to the surface to greet us with a smile — 'Here I Am!' Those with an interest in Deity, the Divine in all things, will rejoice in this work; and for those who have yet to imbibe such sweet nectar, a real treat is in store for you!"

Thom F. Cavalli, Ph.D., Author of *Alchemical Psychology: Old Recipes for Living in a New World* and *Embodying Osiris: the Secrets of Alchemical Transformation*. CavalliBooks.com

"These poems are profound on many levels of feeling and reflection. They speak directly to the soul!"

Kate Hamilton, Author of "Funeral Blog" and Managing Director of Mourningcross Bereavement Pins

"Douglas' poems are deliciously intimate and invitational! Like Rumi, they gift us with a fresh, at times delightfully surprising, and always renewing perspective on our lives. A new and vital Energy now has a hitherto unopened door through which to enter!"

Susan Negley, Jungian Analyst at Susan
Clements Negley, San Antonio, Texas, and
Author of *Coniunctio Gastronomique: Reflections on
the Process of Individuation in Culinary Terms*

"The power and beauty of this body of work! Doug Gillette's poems reveal his extraordinary gifts for counseling, consoling, and inspiring. His 'illuminations' express directly his passionate soul, and realize an arresting and wise balance between that soul and his prodigious intellect!"

Jack Herman, Chicago lawyer

"These poems are word wizardry! They are direct communications from the Beloved!"

Shannon O'Neill, MA Social Work, Adjunct
Professor at Western Carolina University

"These lyrical illuminations enlighten the depths of everyday experience and awaken our sleeping sense to the fantastic beauty lying just beyond the edges of our ordinary perception.

No, more than that! Doug's poems are filled with images of our much-dreaded passage into the Beyond. They also proclaim the promise of our entrance into incredible Beauty, Forgiveness, and brilliant Transformation. His answer to the quest for eternal life is to trust the gift of mythic imagination to introduce us to dimensions of supernatural Beauty exceeding all our wildest expectations! These illuminations are a bold venture into the affirmation of life after death! Do your soul a favor and feast on the fulfillment of that joyful destiny Doug's poems invite you to!"

Rev. Don Jones (deceased), Pastor in The Disciples of Christ Church, past Chairman of the Mankind Project USA Elders, and Author of *Wisdom for the Journey* and *Hunger for Wholeness*

"Douglas M. Gillette's comprehensive and profound collection of poetic 'illuminations' echo the author's discovery and faithful confirmation of an inherently endowed divine Grace hidden below the surface of suffering. Gillette has infused his breathtaking enlightenment of the inner-beyond in a volume that reflects his deep and sincere wish to share his penetrating insights with the reader. Starting from our need to cope with crises, he takes us through an exalted transformation into an astounding state of awareness where bliss is pervasive.

"*At the Thresholds of Elysium: Lyrical Illuminations for Lifting Spirit into Bliss* wants to be your guidebook for a journey headed toward Elysium or Heaven by any other name, which Gillette reveals to be the source of a boundless, omnipresent love. The author premises that any mortal has the potential to transform from a creature of Nature's biological imperatives into a spirit-being capable of learning to operate in a transcendent realm where blissful freedom is paramount.

Juxtaposing contrasting experiences, representing loss and victory over life's challenges, his poetics forge an illuminated path that leads one out of pain to the validation of one's spiritual quest.

"Beautiful thoughts, uplifted with emotional sensitivity and kindness, are the author's vehicles heading toward the portal of a divine Reality. But getting there requires the courage to delve deep, to become aware and awaken within our own awe-inspiring, selfless core. From his perspective these vehicles perfected by ancient seers were designed to guide humans to higher consciousness. Employing his expansive erudition of mythic symbolism, divine concepts, and dream language, the tools Gillette offers us are the philosophies and beliefs of ancient seers who embarked on this course long before modern empiricism took control of the assessment of Reality.

"Now, we, the readers, living under the dome of science and technology, are challenged to shine our own inner light upon the immediate dangers we face in order to cross into a hidden spiritual Reality. Therein, Gillette's poems evoke the verity of what superficial minds dismiss. He dresses his observations in the robe of forbearance declaring that any and all sufferings, from maddening memories to inconsolable grief, may be overcome. By believing, exploring and resonating with the loving, blissful Reality of the divine beyond, he empowers us to experience the redemption of becoming more than we can imagine, the blissful embodiment of divine love."

Harvey Kraft, Spiritual Archaeologist and award-winning Author of *The Buddha from Babylon: the lost History and Cosmic Vision of Siddhartha Gautama* and the novel *The Waker: Portal of Perfect Light*

Other Books by Douglas M. Gillette

The Shaman's Secret: The Lost Resurrection Teachings of the Ancient Maya

Primal Love: Reclaiming Our Instincts for Lasting Passion

King, Warior, Magician, Lover: Rediscovering the Archetypes of the Mature Masculine*

The King Within: Accessing the King in the Male Psyche*

The Warrior Within: Accessing the Knight in the Male Psyche*

The Magician Within: Accessing the Shaman in the Male Psyche*

The Lover Within: Accessing the Lover in the Male Psyche*

*Co-authored with Dr. Robert Moore, Ph.D.

At
the Thresholds of
Elysium

Lyrical Illuminations
for Lifting Spirit into
Bliss

Douglas M. Gillette,
M.A.R.S., M-Div.

At the Thresholds of Elysium

Lyrical Illuminations for Lifting Spirit into Bliss

Douglas M. Gillette, M.A.R.S., M-Div.

Published by
DouglasGilletteCreations

First published in 2016 by
Printed in the United States of America

Library of Congress Cataloging-in-Publication Data
Gillette, Douglas M.

At the Thresholds of Elysium: Lyrical Illuminations for Lifting Spirit into Bliss

Inspiration   General Spirituality

ISBN 9780692771648

For Dora

You chase your dreams into the future you
and God are making,
as once upon a time you danced with skittish
birds and whirling maple seeds.
May all that is most authentically you come
to full fruition, my daughter,
in this life and in eternity.

11-18-16

*For Bob,
with much appreciation
and honouring of you
the person, your life
trajectories and processes.*

"In my Father's House are many places for you to
live.
If that were not true, I would have told you."

The Gospel of John 14: 2

*your mind and heart,
and your companioning.
Much affection always,
Doug*

Contents

Hierophanies   25

Nature, Which Is Always More than That   81

Ghosts and Shadows   261

Reflections in a Splintered Mirror   333

Sublimations   381

Metamorphoses   427

Lifting Spirit into Bliss   483

Bliss into Infinity   517

Essay   527

Acknowledgments

Before all of those many people to whom I am deeply indebted for the realization of this project is my daughter Dora, who has been my primary listener and reader and, indeed, almost always the first person to respond to the illuminations as they gained written form. Dora has been a thoughtful critic, as well as helping me with the editing in general, and with decisions about which poems to include in the collection and which to leave out. She has also been a tireless researcher in a number of areas. I would also like to thank my wife Olga for her similar contributions. In addition, I am grateful to the Reverend Donald Jones for being an early and continuing supporter of the work, and for writing the first review. I would also like to thank Robert Williams, Felice Bassuck, and Barry Koren for also being early readers and careful and appreciative commentators, as well as Jesse Ivory, Director of the Emeritus Program at Oakton Community College, for her nurturing of the work, including her contribution to arranging for one of the first public readings of the illuminations. Similar thanks go to Mike O'Brien. Of course, I deeply appreciate my audiences, particularly many of my students, who heard the illuminations for the first time in my classes, yet also in the context of other venues. I am also indebted to Weston Riesche of SEO Solutions, who worked with me to design, update, and maintain my website, and who helped me to finalize the book cover. I am greatly indebted and enormously grateful to my first reviewers, from all walks of life, who wrote beautiful and insightful assessments of *At the Thresholds of Elysium* when it was still in manuscript form, and whose comments appear on the back cover and in the first pages of this published edition. And I am particularly indebted to Steven Herrmann, Ph.D. for his panoramic and incisive commentary, which can be found immediately after my concluding essay.

As well, I am profoundly grateful for the work that the Amazon CreateSpace and Kindle teams have done in actualizing the published embodiment of this volume.

Foreword

This collection of "lyrical illuminations" is an intensely personal way for me to express what I believe are our common human experiences in the midst of Nature and of our own natures, as we move through the "seasons of the soul" en route to realizing ourselves as Spirit. For me, ideally this is an unfolding process of gradual "divinization," of a lifting up of who and what we are toward greater and ever more inclusive oneness with Beauty, Truth, and Goodness—always and finally, all-encompassing Love. That, for me, is God.

My own life (so far 67 years of it) has led me to a number of specific views, as well as to an overarching perspective, both of which these illuminations attempt to express. I won't suggest that these views are true for everyone in every detail or at every stage of their lives, either here or Hereafter. What I can say is that within my own life experiences they lift burdens and clear emotional and thought-full spaces. Some of them guide me through dark and narrow passages. Many of them loft me into blissful states of awareness—into environments of hope, faith, wonder, peace, gratitude, and awe. To whatever extent these illuminations might speak to you, and, in some cases, perhaps *for* you, I hope that they may be affirming, insightful, heart-healing, intellectually stimulating, and enabling of a compelling and joyous en-spiriting.

One way I could describe the overall perspective that I have reached about my own journey through Nature and, as I believe, beyond it, is that it represents a kind of multi-dimensional "Neo-platonic Christian realism." I've become convinced that within each of us there is Light beyond light and Life above life — that there is much more to all of us than we are normally in-touch with — illimitable heights and ultimately unfathomable depths. I think we all have had at least inklings of further identities that we also are — perhaps especially in moments of stress and crisis, when our usual assumptions about ourselves, others, and the nature of reality become seriously challenged, significantly shifted, or even come dramatically unglued. These moments can be exhilarating, terrifying, or both at once. But it is in these moments, I think, that we are drawn closest to our Source, our Sustenance, and our final Destination at the infinite Divine. Unquestionably, I do have a streak of Gnostic darkness running through me like an underground river. The darkness with which we are undeniably confronted is very real for me, yet is always resolved in breath-taking vistas of Light. (For those who might wish to explore more specifics of my world view, I have included a short essay at the conclusion of the illuminations.)

In these and other ways, I think of myself as residing in the neighborhood of the Apostle Paul, Cardinal Nicholas of Cusa, C.S. Lewis, J.R.R. Tolkien, C.G. Jung, the Islamic Sufis, the Hegelians, the Pythagoreans, the Neoplatonists, the Hermeticists, the great medieval Muslim theologian Ibn al-'Arabi, the ancient Egyptians, the Maya, and of all those from all spiritual as well as secular-scientific perspectives who have powerfully felt the delicious and frightening mysteriousness of our human situation and that inconceivably vast Reality in which we are wholly and inextricably immersed, at this moment and forever, and which we ourselves embody, think, and feel. "Salvation" for me is recalling this in the midst of our earthly lives, and, through that recalling, moving beyond these lives to higher and brighter expressions of the Self—thereby "lifting spirit into Bliss." Thus, according to my own lights, I am what I would describe as an inclusivistic Christian Universalist.

A note about organization. The illuminations are grouped into eleven major themes, from a Prologue and Summonings (how we are often called to adventures of the spirit), through a series of "ordinary" and extraordinary experiences—Hierophanies; Nature, Which Is Always More than That; Paeans, Prayers, and Divine Considerations; Ghosts and Shadows; Reflections in a Splintered Mirror; Sublimations—moving toward a gradual, and sometimes sudden, culmination in experiences of exaltation in the Divine—Metamorphoses; Lifting Spirit into Bliss; and Bliss into Infinity. In these and other ways, the illuminations unfold a kind of "narrative of salvation" for the individual soul.

Let me conclude by offering the following invitations and wishes.

These illuminations are for:

Everyone who has ever been struck down by darkness, and everyone who has been lifted into Light;

Everyone who has felt confined by life as it has been given, and everyone who has sensed a vastness just beyond it;

Everyone who has been plunged into heartbreak, and everyone who knows they have been rescued;

Everyone who has wished for a happy ending, and everyone who is unable to;

Everyone who believes in a transcendent Goodness, and everyone who can't.

I wish for every reader-listener:

To feel that they have connected with, and found an honoring of, a wide range of the most impactful experiences of their lives;

As a result, to feel that they have been seen, heard, and validated in their human-ness;

To feel confirmed in their sense that they are vaster and more expansive than their daily lives have been able to reveal;

To feel inspired and lifted by Beauty, Truth, Goodness, and Love;

To feel that they have been found…and freed!

Peace to you, and all Blessings,
Doug Gillette

Prologue

A Flood of Sun and Thunder

That sweet-and-tart and disinhibited vanishing
drops back and back forever,
and I, running or dancing, push off from my own
earth,
and loft into this far-flung exultation
until I thin to nothingness, extinguished in a
boundary-less crescendoing —
then, astounded, reconvene with all my joys about
me ringing —
those and that which I have loved and those and
what I did not — all alighted with me
in a flood of sun and thunder.

2-24-13

Magical Enactments

Let us move through the world as if it were
an unceasing living magic.
Let us be becomings of that, as if we were
ourselves instantiations
in human form of just such superlative
enchantments. My experience
of my own life is that
it is, from before it began until some time
indeterminately past it,
one great, and many small, fantastic magical
enactments.

12-7-15

I Believe

I believe that Deity is guiding us, all along this
press-ganged voyage, through storms,
becalming seas, and every form of danger —
this, until our port is reached: some uncharted isle,
dark with trees, where evening never falls
and it is always summer.

11-11-13

Summonings

A Lullaby of Light

I need to hear a lullaby, a recitation or a chant that
hushes into quiet joy all hurtful things
and strife.
I need to hear redemption, a song of reassurance or
a triumphal paean, that soothes the pain of
clashing wills,
that sieves the dregs of evil, that cherishes the
good, the beautiful, a music that makes all things
calm and bright.

I need to hear a song of healing for all creatures in
their existential fright, a symphony of highest
silence
which transforms all things, and makes them fresh
and clean and right in some dream-time space
above
where hooves and claws, opening palms and
pounding fists are smoothed
into a lullaby of Light.

10-11-15

Something in Addition

I

What have you seen nickering between your toes
from underneath,
shadowing the soles of your feet?

Haven't you found that stygian void disquieting?

Have you noticed the gleam in the deep of your
eye,
just past the iris, within the pool of the pupil?

Who do you think that might be, watching you,
biding, biding?

Haven't you yet felt a Mind behind your mind,
inside I mean,
flank-by-flank, intimate with dendritic lightning?

Don't you think something in addition to naiveté
and daylight?

II

Have you seen that glittering nimbus that wreathes
your cheeks, and blows like wildfire through your
hair?

I have witnessed it when you're running and
laughing, flushed with summer or snowy
afternoons.

Haven't you noticed something bright and otherworldly around
your eyes when you're suddenly surprised and delighted?

I have seen it when your joy is full — say, listening to music, up late in your room.

Haven't you felt your imagination glow, wrap around you like a fairy robe,
when you're experimenting with make-up, or reading a beloved book?

What do you think you look like in such moments?

Don't you think something considerably more than a creature that will wither and die?

I do.

9-26-15

Inconsolably Passed

In grief, the absent person is heart-rendingly
present — present to the spirit, but matterless —

and will rise upon your solitude like an implacable
dread of fossilized crinoids or trilobites —

once thriving, now mineralized — worse, for once
having been human, yet shot-through and
paralyzed

by that obdurate "never again" of Nature's massive
and unimportunable factness.

The who and what that lived beside you and was
internalized,

will never re-manifest or come back from that
blotting of time's unidirectional consignment.

Messages conveying continuity initially seem
welcome, but the messengers will drop
lifeless at your limen.

He or she you loved has sunk to irretrievable
depths of, say, the Akashic Record,[1] or the
undelimited Psyche.

---

[1] Akashic Record: In Theosophy, the collective Record of all
thoughts, feelings, actions, and events

Memories will flicker like sun through wind-
thrashed trees.
But such things are mockeries of the aliveness
you shared — now inconsolably passed.

8-26-15

All My Fears

I have raced above the winter trees, white
wastelands of shorn and broken arborage
inhabited by rabbits, wolves, and deer,

been dazzled by the flash of diamond snows,
laid down for miles and miles,
frozen creeks and streams,

heaped, frost-crisped brambles, desiccated
greens standing blond and stiffly
in a breezeless freeze.

I have listened vainly for the rustling of wings,
the brittle shifting of spindly feet,
a warble or a cheap,

hurtling through a crackling, cloudless blue-above
toward a rendezvous with some shattering
figuration of the sun, and all my fears.

12-1-13

The Light of Heaven

I have seen the light of Heaven pass across the
human face
in moments of wonder, joy, and deep tranquility.

I have seen it gleam in the eyes, sparkle on the
teeth, stream
through the hair in autumn winds or on a summer
breeze.

I have seen it drop the jaw, startle up tears, furrow
laugh lines,
part the lips, relax the forehead, flush the cheeks.

I have seen it bestowed in the myriad cloaks of
Nature. I have
seen it too descend on the spirit as a supernatural
peace.

However it comes, from whatever quarter and no
matter how
fleeting, within such instants I have seen the person

rendered immaculate and redeemed.

7-21-14

With Every Other Each Thing

In the Great Fullness[2] abide all things—everything
that walks, slithers,
swims or has wings—also even stranger and more
wonderful things.

Each is what it is at its extreme. At the same time,
each is seamlessly
blended with every other each thing.

In the Great Fullness is a limitless Light and Life
higher and brighter
than any yet dreamed.

Each thing in the Fullness lives in this world which
presently seems,
but diminutively, compromised, and most
dramatically dimmed.

When we are swept back into that Fullness, we and
all things, reliving
within us all we have been, all will be changed in
less than a twinkling

---

[2] The Great Fullness: In Gnosticism, the primordial "Pleroma"
of the Divine in which all things dwell before, during, and
after their actualization in the manifested, or existentiated,
world.

and sing—each as what it is at its extreme, and
seamlessly blended with
every other each thing.

6-5-14

You Shall Not Be Forsaken

For all who mourn lost opportunities with
parents, spouses, partners, children;
for all whose hearts are breaking for the harm
they've done — miniscule altercations
or wholesale carnage; for all who grieve self-
inflicted wounds; for all who couldn't give
their best because of damaged childhoods, or
of their world views or their circumstances
suffered insurmountable limitations;
for all whose lives have been cut short, or who've
been stifled in their mental development,
or nipped in the bud by some alternative
restriction;
for all who've been ignored, abused, bullied,
or made victims of cruelty or injustice; for all who
stand witness to their progressive irrelevance…

I say:

It's alright. It's all right.

You have yet other lives to live.

And you have never been, nor shall you ever be
forsaken.

10-11-14

Parousia

A trumpet blast or ram's horn shatters the
drowsing atmosphere!
Atoms burst, flame, then iridescent, melt like
scented paraphine!

Rocks grind, cast up vermillion dust which ignites
a general conflagration!
Earthquakes level everything the human being has
constructed or achieved!

I ask, "When will this dreaded termination of our
tenure come to pass, the payment for our deeds?"

"That parousia,"[3] answered she in winding, bright-
hued fabrics, "messianic advent, Osiris rising
gigantic, green,

occurs each moment that Siddhartha, deep within
the million things, touches Earth with two-fold
fingertips, and all that is

cries out together, "'I bear witness! What now
exists or ever has been is Deity or nirvana!'"

"Yes," say I, "You have described us exactly."

---

[3] Parousia: In Christianity, the coming of the "Presence" of
God in/as Jesus-the-Christ at the end of the world.

She: "And He has lived enough of this!
Touch the Earth. Now wake up and
know eternal bliss!"

4-7-09

In Awareness of Celestial Forms

In awareness of celestial forms or archetypes,
however these are named,
I see eternal Beauty envisaged in my daughter's
years of eight —

the shining eyes, the party dress, coiled hair atop
her mane, pressing
outward from some hidden-inner, flesh conformed
to spirit —

the former fugitive, Dorita passing through a mist
or prism which casts
her as illusory enchantment with something of
misgiving — this,

by means of arcane images, her transiently
inhabiting these. Then that
searches out another, and abandons her to
blotching flesh and wrinkles.

Thus is Nature fickle, and as Plotinus[4] guessed, that
which proves itself unfaithful,

---

[4] Plotinus (205-270 C.E.): The great Egypto-Hellenic Platonist
who initiated the Neoplatonic movement which powerfully
influenced major currents of theological and philosophical
thought in Paganism, Judaism, Christianity, and Islam, as well
as providing inspiration for many of the seminal theorists of
the Scientific Revolution and Modernity.

whatever it presumes, does not merit the best of
nomenclature or titles

of highest eminence. Yet even if I were willing to
concede that Nature's beauty,
gracing Dora, manifests no more than matter's
restless rummaging —

in other words, its own as Dora's insufficiencies,
still, above its scurry it might
reveal some vital aspect of Divinity — say, the
Maker's Mind, immobile.

Yet how can it finally be maintained that static
unchanging ranks higher
than animation, plasticity, personhood, or
aliveness?

No. Dora, as well as Nature's beauty, which in her I
say reposes, her very
Ground and Source-as-she more than adequately
apprises.

That is You, O God. However, You are not at all,
nor worth a thought,
without her self-disclosure.

12-18-04

All of These

The fiery globe of Sol[5] glaring, yellow as an
incandescent bulb,
ascended through a swoon of mist-strewn
phosphorescent gauze

across the fields, gilding these with otherworldly
ambers, greens.
Untangling from

the limbs of trees, he floated up into that day-lit
vault of self-wrought
dreams,

declared with fanfare of the stirring birds his
freedom and his majesty.
I was present there. I saw, and knew that I was all
of these.

6-9-15

---

[5] Sol: Ancient Latin name for the god of the sun

Hierophanies[6]

---

[6] Hierophanies: "Divine Self-disclosures" through the forms and dynamics of the existentiated world.

The Manner of My Transit

Silence reigns in that most intimate and
hermetically sealed abyss
between what we know and what we are permitted
to speak,
mute as those carved stone lips
of Egyptian statues, recursively smiling, lush and
smooth, as if they could be kissed.

Beyond individuality and its necessities, these are
unresponsive. He or she depicted
has been withdrawn from the realm of that and
this,
is now fulfilled, super-human, sublimed and
blissed.

I myself have fallen into that fantastic masslessness
between my essence and existence,
then reappeared on one side or the other, amnesiac
of what has intervened
and the manner of my transit.

7-11-16

Angelic Messenger

Should some angelic messenger, claws of bronze,
black-bristled,
with iron arms like Assyrian warriors carved in
relief,

bash the hinges from my bedroom door, seize me
at some moment
of extremity, collapsed in tears and grief,

or drag me from beneath those buckthorn
hedgerows Jesus preached,
and haul me to his Master's wedding feast,[7]

I would kick and scream, shake whatever fist I'd
left at his feathered
face and beak, challenge him with my perplexity,

charge him as a thief. He would no doubt laugh, or
roar, stripe me
with his tongue of fire, shot out between his teeth.

Noting my condition then, he might sit,
physicianish,
at my bedside, bury claws into the mattress
springs, glossolalic,[8] begin to sing

---

[7] Wedding Feast: From the New Testament, the Gospel of
Luke, chapter 14, verses 15-24
[8] Glossolalia: In early Christianity, the phenomenon known as
"speaking in tongues," or otherworldly languages

some Word deeper than my bewilderment and
seething,
loosening those losses which have embittered me.
Then he'd raise great rainbow wings.

I would shout, "I've turned my back on God and
all His crowd of griffins,
snakes, and sphinxes! I don't believe in anything!

Nor will I yield to you or go with you to your
euphemistic 'wedding feast'!"
His beard would quake, azure as the sea. He would
uproot me

then, from bed or hedgerow, and pronounce my
doom. He'd thunder,
"All are hoped, even those that never do!" And
he'd reveal

sliding films of skin across the eyes — saurian, I
would guess, nictitating
membranes, like those of serpents or of basilisks.

And I would go with him.

7-5-02

Golden Serpents

Golden serpents glide upright on tips of
languorous
flickering tails, wave-like bodies subtly glowing,
through cinnamon scented trees at dusk, five of
these elated by an atom's breadth alone
above the aromatic earth. Issue they a whispered
swishing sound, passing through thigh-high
grasses, wearing their antiquity with eerie grace
and preternatural severity, mildness.
Eyes wide, they pierce the humid green, dripping
lushness of their woods and glades, and shiver
toward the Tree of God-like Knowledge and the
Tree of Immortality, in suspended animation
at the Center, both festooned with rampant vines
bearing pharmacological fruit
entwined with almond-offering boughs. There they
float-and-feed, and simultaneously renew their
Wisdom and their Youth.

Upright golden serpents are part of our identities.
That part of us has never left the Garden.

That part of us has never lied, nor shall it end in
death.

12-2-15

Dumbfounded

He came at us, clattering down that steep descent
from what's above to our own well-worn level,
wearing sun-forged grieves and breastplate,
shield strapped across his back, freshly risen from
his burial,

his long hair coursing in the wind he'd raised by
the rushing hither of his flaming shade,
his beard ablaze, eyes on fire from the light he'd
been, now dimmed so we could see his face.

When he spoke, it sounded like the warbled cooing
of a hundred doves, mooting to us both foreboding
and, it seemed, some Elysianic[9] joy.

We summoned Ephialtes[10] from among the men, a
seer, to interpret for us the eerie speech of the
deceased — Patroclus',[11] Achilles' lover, newly slain,
now here before us. It goes without saying

we were rattled, kept our eyes fixed upon the
phantom, lapping up and down minutely

---

[9] Elysianic: Having to do with Elysium, the ancient Greek term
for Heaven or Paradise

[10] Ephialtes: A seer or oracle in the Greek army during the
Trojan War.

[11] Patroclus: In the Trojan War, the lover of the greatest
Greek warrior, Achilles. Patroclus' death brought Achilles
back into the War, which contributed significantly to the
ultimate Greek victory.

above the ground, soles of his feet six inches from
the sand. He looked at us somewhat vaguely, as
if

he both registered our presence yet saw beyond
us, with an expression fierce and quiet at the same
time, and subtly altering, as though his
countenance might take whatever shape he wished.

Ephialtes arrived. Achilles had not been found —
undoubtedly weeping somewhere further up the
beach. The seer abruptly halted when he saw our
oddly lustrous visitor, then inched

forward toward him, leaning nearer, and closed his
eyes to concentrate on that birdsong slipping
through the glimmering lips. After a few minutes,
he backed away, opened his eyes, turned to us,
and said, "Word for word:

'I'm better off here than there with you,
though you'll know for yourselves in an instant.
The hallowed halls of Troy will fall,
but with them your own civilization.
Thus it always is, has been, and will be.
The energies we employ in acquisition
must count for something, though
at the moment, that eludes me.
Send each other to the deaths we all must die!
In the end, there's only peace and reconciliation.'

"That's everything," Ephialtes said.
Patroclus, or I should say, his image, projected who
knows how, vanished in a gilded shower. His light
diffused into the shadows of the night,
and we were left dumbfounded.

1-19-15

Narcissus

That green stone-lined pool in which Narcissus[12]
gazed, its verges staved by sedge and unbreezed
reeds,
shadowed in places, made opaque, by thickly
woven canopies bending toward the glaze, caused
him to see

an almost motionless reflection of his face. He fell
in-love with that, believing it was the operation
of some stranger
who dwelled within the pool, who'd glided up to
meet him at a break between the planes.

He felt himself go over wholly to that set of jaw, the
gleaming teeth, the kindness of those lidless liquid
eyes,
the ghostly ivory of the skin, the chestnut hair
lightly stirred by currents he could not feel.
Paralyzed,

---

[12] Narcissus: In ancient Greek mythology, the son of the blue
Nymph Leiriope and the River-god Cephisus, after rejecting all
would-be lovers, both male and female, fell in-love with his
reflection in a pond. In the original myth, Narcissus killed
himself with a dagger when he realized he could not
consummate his love with "the youth" in the pond.

at the crack of doom and wonderment, he was will-
less, with neither strength nor wish to move.
In that state he died. Many who've heard
Narcissus' tale have condemned him as a self-
ensorcelled fool.

But what I think Narcissus saw was the face he
wore before his fall into the world of space and
matter.
Which one of us, confronted by our Higher Selves,
would not go suddenly still as death and waste
away, enchanted?

4-12-14

Light around the Meat

I have seen the person dwindle.
I have seen the person cease.

I have seen the person change
from personality to meat.

I have seen the person vanish,
and I've seen light around the meat.

8-22-09

Upon My Resurrection

If I could see you now as you see me,
I know I would be ravished by the sight —
upheld by light, a ruffling breeze about
your hair, your eyes moist, even kinder

than before, bright with knowledge I
have yet to gain, that face and flesh I loved
somehow golden, yet unchanged,

the clothes you wore, your mannerisms,
your way of listening and speaking,
although altered, still, thank God, the same.

I would fall in-love with you all over again,
even though I've never stopped feeling that,
as I did first in my apartment, gently, quietly,
when you came to cook and clean, the magic

of our first home together in Houston, our
daughter as fruition of that pact we made to
back each other up through thick and thin,
through health and sickness,

wealth and poverty, no matter what the cost,
to raise our daughter well, to respect each other
and cherish each other's strengths as well as
imperfections.

How more than glad I'll be to see you, touch you, smell you, hear you, taste you, make love with you again upon my resurrection!

11-18-13

Phidias' Zeus

There are many ways of loving God, in aspects
actualized
and ethereal, finitized as incorporeal, within our
grasp
and also past the sum of our capacities for
abstraction.

I myself need double vision when it comes to Deity,
and, I think,
God is more than happy to supply my aptitude for
being — as well, my yearning for transcendence of
it.

With this in mind, I wish to say the following: It is
not true,
    as some have claimed, that Phidias[13] was an
idolater.
He possessed an insuperable view of the Divine,
from my vantage,

yet believed that God could nonetheless be represented in
such a manner, on such a scale, and with such
evocative an
out-flowing of nobility in His visage,

---

[13] Phidias: The famous 5th century B.C.E. Greek sculptor
whose statue of Zeus became a focus for a more elevated and
majestic conception of the Greek High-God.

that this image of That Which ultimately escapes all efforts at
expression, even thought, might still be rendered, and with
that rendering, inspire wonderment and awe —
appropriate

emotions when drawing close to absolute Mystery and Love.
Phidias accomplished this without suggesting in any way that
God could be mistaken for wood, gold, or polished ivory, or that his human craft

might do any more than hint at that paradoxical all-surpassing
Maximum and most Intimate Reality. Phidias labored mightily
in his shop on the plains of Olympia. There he designed that titanic

icon — sawed, planed, chiseled, hammered the wood, cut and
wrought the sheets of gold, carved and oiled the ivory —
yes, of course, for his financial benefit and for everlasting accolades.

But the finished product, as I've suggested, testified to a vision of
the Deity so charged with power, and with

benignant beauty —
a vision which, effulgent, issued from some lofty
sky-bright reach within that craftsman's

anagogic[14] mind, there can be no question of his
sincerity. Phidias
knew, as perhaps artists only may, that God is,
irreducibly, invisible,
and may not be tracked

much further than our senses, especially our
hearing and our sight.
However, any image which invites the human
species in the direction
of transfiguration,

and lifts us thus with apparitions and unearthly
intimations to higher
realms of Consciousness and Light, surely
constitutes authentic, hence
most truthful, Self-disclosure, or hierophany.

1-28-09

---

[14] Anagogic: "ascending" or "world-transcending"

The Transformation of Aquinas

Aquinas[15] near the end, like an initiate into ancient
mysteries,
glimpsed something gliding between oil lamps'
gleam

and moving mirrors, such that he exclaimed,
"Whatsoever I have
witnessed recently renders all conceptions upon
which
I have labored, straw."

He did not elaborate. Yet one may conjecture that
what he saw,
beyond discursive intellect or words of any species,

was identical with that which Plato grasped in
company of Diotima,[16]
or I myself have seen in moments of lofty pause
and exaltation,

---

[15] St. Thomas Aquinas (1227-1274 C.E.): The highly influential
Catholic theologian who plausibly reconciled important
aspects of the thought-systems of Aristotle and Plato with a
Christian world view.

[16] Diotima: The famous female mystic, teacher of Socrates,
who appears in Plato's "Symposium" dialogue instructing
Socrates in the methods for transcending the material world
by using beautiful objects and persons as stepping stones into
the spiritual realm in which Beauty Itself may be experienced
directly.

in the Presence of which every thing is shown to be
precisely what it is,
and all, light and shadow, lacking error, without
flaw,

unspeakable Goodness—beauteous, wondrous,
true, with such thrill
the soul experiences unexpected confirmation,
and the rolling heart ceases its careening.

12-17-04

There It Is!

John on Patmos[17] was correct: that's exactly where
it is!
He was pacing his cell, slyly spied from out the
corner
of his eye some magnificent shining orb!
He ducked his head, moustache, straggling beard,
turned
one-eighty slowly — not the feet, just the head —
ogled them,
seven brass lamps, oil
flashing wide like suns up close…right there in his
living
room, ten feet distant maybe. Whole worlds
opened,
whatever lies beyond, previously only supposed —
Heaven, Hell. It left him reeling. Muhammad some
years
later paused on a dusty street in Mecca before
someone's
garden wall, focused on the brickwork, stepped
forward,
cocked his head and halted. His eyes snapped tight.
He slipped, without moving, through the gate, a
finger
raised to shush the jinn, and commenced a state of

---

[17] John of Patmos: The ostensible author of the New
Testament book of Revelation.

world-
eclipsing otherness, stunned, then spoke:"There
it is...Paradise and the Pit...all that is or ever shall
be...
between the tips of my toes and that garden wall!
Over it,
sheer nothingness!" I myself, awake three nights
and
days, beheld a golden disk, eight feet in diameter,
set on
edge just beyond my kitchen, upright on the
floor...
a computer of sorts—chips, circuitry, codes,
rivulating
toward the center—all trajectories of thought,
dimensions
without number, love, death, resurrection,
fashioned
with solidity, yet imaginal, right there past the
cutting board!

12-12-08

Corners

Look here now!
There's a corner here,
and down there
there's a whole universe,
populated, jostling—
sights, sounds, smells, waiting!
And over there too, another corner—

like fanning pages of a book.
An edge flies by; you glimpse a page—
another edge, another page,
edge/page, edge/page.
Then it's so fast, it's continuous.
Then you see what God sees.
Amazing!

1-12-12

In Deepest Love

In deepest love we know each other as inviolable
infinity itself although
in animal masquerade, wild as wind, enclosed by
supra-natural auras,
and that each of us represents a break in time and
space,
or a well of light which plunges down forever,
bottomless, beyond
the reach of give-and-take or arrangements
of any artifice or making. In infinite regress from
actuality to essence,
or turned the other way,
at every stage we wear our lustrous otherworldly
faces. We know each
other as priceless individual beings who cannot be
replaced,
and as well, that radiant Singularity at the core of
things, diaphanous,
all-illuminate.
In such love as I have for you, I sometimes feel
myself abate. And
in that love, Divinity Itself becomes
both obvious and annihilate.

2-7-13

Idolater

Grunts, profanities, blood, heave of muscle,
sleepless nights,
the forms of God stand forth from nothingness—
pencil, saw, spatula, plaster, skinned knuckles,
wounded hands,
bending, twisting, molecular percussioning,
the faces of Divinity hierophanize from fathomless
immensities,
find embodiment by means of this—
this sculptor or musician's suffering and elations,
her sinews,
her will, her deep envisionings.

What hath she wrought with such integrity of
purpose?
Not God surely—yet not not He.

11-27-04

Through You

Through you the Infinite breathes Beauty and
Goodness
into my most intimate depths, where fear and hope
arise,
hippogryph[18] and angel, nightmare and bliss, and,
in your
disguise, consumes me in self-naughting fire.

11-18-12

---

[18] Hippogryph: In ancient Greek mythology, a being half horse
and half gryphon (a bird-like creature)

Ancient of the Ancients

Unforeseen, he apparates on the instant, bearing
the moon on his shoulder,
left, I think, as if it were a bird, parrot or a raven, or
he slipped it smoothly
over his face like a mask.

I couldn't be sure which. But, before that, I got a
peak at his face—pocked,
tarnished like corroded copper, wisps of cloud
about his countenance,
which, like clear air cast

across that nightscape, somehow manufactured
ghosts, discharged them from
his prosopon or cloak, and sent them rushing
through the atmosphere,
unlooked for and unbidden. That antique traveler,

ancient of ancients, stood within his self-made shaft
of light, aloft, or edgewise,
sharp-tusked, and cleaved that gulf of silver-
shrouded woods, wild with
shadow, thick with unicorn and centaur.[19]

He gestured, open-handed, steadied that smokeless
lamp upon his shoulder,
or removed it from his face, so that I could see him

---

[19] In ancient Greek mythology, a creature half human and half
horse

more clearly. He stepped
toward me, spoke like summer thunder,

"You, come with me!" crooked his penumbraed
forefinger, compressing vacuums
rippling over dreaming water of a frozen pond or
stream. I was drawn up into
a gusty sort of stillness, resistlessly enchanted.

What I'd been and labored to achieve was
instantaneously extinguished in that
bog or matrix from which it had once arisen — yet
never would outlive its
cherishing in that Homeland of his Vastness.

6-17-09

The Third Person

When a child speaks of what we recognize as him-
or her-self
in the third person,
who or what is the "I" which references the child as
if it were,
and not, him or her?
Who is it that takes the third person as an object of
its subjectivity
yet knows the child's inner needs and purposes?
Who speaks for the ego not yet fully identified with
that being
in particular, as if it were
only gradually incarnating and hasn't fully got its
bearings?

Someone does. Someone uses the third person. To
speak in the
third person requires a first person
who is in the background, and assumed. There is
no object without
a subject, and equally, vice versa.
To have "our own" identities demands a subject
that is not us.
To become recognizable to ourselves
we need to be the objects of someone else's
subjectivity, a kind
of subjectivity that knows us before
we know ourselves. What's more, a subjectivity,

because it speaks
for us to our custodians, that is not our parents'.

Who or what could fill that bill? I can think of only
one.

8-25-12

Between Seven and Eight

My daughter's smile, her laughter, the lightning in
her eyes,
or sudden fright,
the fineness of her forming nose, her lips, her
squalls of tears,
sometimes terrors of the night...
her lilting voice, upon occasion vamp, that mole
that ornaments
her shoulder on the right,
marking her most supple hide, intimately stamped
and localized,
citing her specifically...
her soul which ever more insistently presents itself
arrived,
yet is still in transit from some phantasmagoric
sky —
this, via that plastic organ of her brain, upwelling
innocence,
which nonetheless thrusts with might and main
against the ossifying
ramparts of the skull, still knitting, which, when
completed, will survive
her earthly life —
she at such time distracted from this dimension of
lit solarity
into a realm of unobstructed gazing...but in the
present still, her creativities,

inspired
narrations, these enablings of the frame by which
she tastes, seeks mastery
of her firmament by increasing
radii,
and circumambulates that Essence at her core,
attempting
in this now and here fulfillment—
yet ever she, nothing more nor could be, within this
phosphorescent haze:
all this and more I hail.

As she embodies, she maintains a close liaison with
her infancy,
now a nearly empty stage upon which she once
played...
lost to her and never, a certain longing to remain at
breast or cradle
mixed with urges to advance as she is able.

For all the grandeur of this in which I know myself
to be dispersed,
immensity beyond enfabling,
if Dora is not the living God personified, what we
endure—daughter,
father—surpassing all restrictions of valuation,

she of infinite worth
precisely as herself, then I care nothing for Divinity,
nor for all these
trumped up orisons and oblations.

2004

Paradise Verging

Sometimes Paradise floods across my earthscape
as a torrent of light. Other times, it rears up
suddenly, motionless, immediate and immanent

in all that is and each particular, as if a curtain
had been rent or a veil had been lifted.

It may creep like liquid fire between the trunks of
trees, like a forest sun quavering toward
the dawn, some molten seepage

from an otherworldly verge that backgrounds what
it isn't—twigs and shadowed leaves.

Or in a clearing when the light is high, it may
brindle like a wall of white, dash alien
brilliance over that which strives,

and hush it back to that indistinctness from which
it soon or late arrived.

It might stave and startle all of this toward where
the sky goes black from glare, and soothe it
into vapor in those waves of heat that come with
day.

I don't know what that is. I call it "Paradise" or "God."
More I cannot say.

8-5-10

The Golden One

The Golden One revolves — golden hair, face,
blazing eyes — cleaves
the Mother's Womb downward, slips savage,
gilded shoulders

like a lion's, or like antelope hips-and-hooves,
through that timeless
labyrinth or passage, and hypostasized with
boldness,

erupts into this byzantine roil of existentiated
things, overturning
golden tables, cups, platters, thrones

in the midst of all this wealth of entities He Himself
has dreamed,
creating by His birth, abruptly or in the course of
eons,

these more than several worlds, plus certain sacred
things — thus
discloses to Himself His Visage, and, as in a lake of
gold

or on a sheet of bronze, contemplates and knows
Himself in the costumes
of these myriads, who in their jubilation praise Him
as He beholds

them as the Golden One Who ever lives, enfolding
them, they within,
Who never dies, so they don't.

12-26-04

I Know You, Megatonned

I know You, megatonned, foliaged,
black with ghosts of ancient dogs and crows.
With sightless eyes that never close
You watch me.

7-9-05

At the Crossing

Upon the threshold of that most inarticulable of
twilights,
dawnings, I'll pause, if permitted, in momentary
consciousness,
feel my heart's final flutter,

and watch stars, moon, sun, all sources of
illumination setting,
that purpling dusk that follows — presently, other
lamps rising into
an unfamiliar heaven.

To what deity or Thee of this will I be praying then,
whose
name will be upon my lips, spoken or echoing in
my interior
when death's clutter

clears, or what mask will be presented to me in
greeting, what
qualities, devotions, failings will be commanding
my obedience when
my face becomes uneven?

Of what will my first sights be staged — idylls,
horrors, commonplaces,
ghosts, gardens, antelope on vast savannahs, fawn-
like creatures, or
none that I could name?

Or, if I should slip through dreams, might some
gigantic man-like
thing with oiled beard and limbs like trees, or a
poetess or witch,
reach out a hand or fin

to me in utter darkness or in a blaze of white, and
see me appointed,
however that might be, unto some location I have
earned, or, more likely,
to which I've undeservedly been raised?

8-14-05

Moments

Why do we have to go on?

I want to go back.

I want to go back to certain moments,
raise my hand, palm open,
and stop or radically slow them.

Memory and photographs are not enough.
I want to go inside those
moments and be there in decelerated
motion,

so slowed that I could live within them
forever, but also watch them,
know every detail as well as the whole,

and value them for what they were really
worth. What they were
really worth is everything holy.

They deserve that—to be valued as absolute,
as worthy of Eternity, as in
themselves equivalent to the Total.

That would be Heaven for me.
I wouldn't want anything more.

Actually, I think that *is* what they were —
the timeless Self-showings of God.

2-23-14

Faith

In the end there is only faith or not, and in
extremity,
that or its absence
becomes urgently personal, as in the hoped-for
survival
of those we love
beyond their material terminations, and my own
wished-to-be continuance
after this "me" has ceased. Or perhaps there's a
detaching
of them and us from who we
were completely, a severance into Buddhist-like
oblivion,
some dropping off into the fantastic.

The thing is this: there comes a time-frame or an
epoch
during which an irreversible
cancelling commences, when the air goes thin,
there's
nothing left to grasp and nothing left to stand on—
no breath, no senses, no sensation
whatsoever,
when we must let go and coast into fathomlessness,
right past Newton, Bohr, Einstein,
on beyond philosophers
and theologians, past race, ethnicity, nation, maybe
even humanity.

Do you believe, in that final exhalation — for
yourself, yet
with more poignancy, for your loved ones —
in Nature's absolute indifference and negation, or
in Deity
and Its Affirmation and Benevolence?
I'm not certain that our fates are any different, no
matter
what might be our stances.
But I for one find vanishment incredible, Nature's
wastefulness
despicable,
and have had impressed upon me in terms I cannot
question
the certainty of our survival.

3-9-13

Most Intimately Alone

After the last theory's thought, the last equation written,
the last symphony played, the last book closed,

I am left to myself, like coelacanth,[20] lizard and worm before me,
to face the hard-edged light of that unclothed

"Showing Forth" which always was exploding beneath my feet,
pressing from behind the screen of loved and loathed,

and now engages all of my attention: that vast Reality and me,
in a place where Nature's noise is merely memory

and I am, if not entirely abandoned, at least in rather full appreciation
of my diminished and untenable position,

teetering at the limit of what is and isn't, myself and total cancellation,
me and that overwhelmingly Alien Other

---

[20] Coelacanth: An ancient armored species of fish, thought to have become extinct until rediscovered in the modern era off the coast of Madagascar.

with Whom I am presently, as it now seems clear
I've always been,
most intimately alone.

4-16-13

By the Heart

There is no final answer for the meaning of the
world.
We will puzzle it out, incompletely, by means of
genes

and life experience. Not only will our answers be
incomplete,
they will be skewed, and several, according to our
moods
or our necessities.

Jesus said that in his Father's House are many
mansions. Indeed!
Muhammad wrote that the Wisdom of his Lord
might not
ever be

fully written, even if the oceans were filled with
ink, and quills
more than plentiful. I think the world as meaning

is infinite, with an infinity of reverberations,
echoes, or Chinese
boxes, one enclosing another, as variously
proposed by mystics

and Georg Cantor.[21] One is left with faith, or not,
and, with it,
values or the lack of these. The secret, if such there
be, is evidently

exceedingly well-hidden, perhaps as Sufis have
suggested, by termless
veils of light and shadow. That's not to say give up,
but
rather, to observe reality,

and live it by the heart, which, in the end or even
most immediately,
alone may understand and, so to speak, know the
truth, and be it.

2-20-11

---

[21] Georg Cantor (1845-1918): The famous mathematician who
demonstrated the existence of a potential infinity of infinities
within "infinity."

Evidently Thriving

I don't say I saw a visible light, but there
was a lightness in the room,
and at the ceiling, or higher up, the feeling
of an open window.

I don't say I heard my mother's voice
audibly, but I did hear her, in my mind.

She said, "Douglas, it's so beautiful over
here! Keep doing what you're doing."

I felt such unrushed happiness.
Incredibly, she was still alive, and evidently
thriving!

4-13-14

Ephemeral Dignities

Heroes, heavy-thighed, predation-boned-and-jointed,
thundered once from under undulating scapulae,
then lifted, light as cirrus clouds or thistle, into the
flagrant air, incendiary decantations, themselves
glowing

like catapulted meteorological events, and issued
far-ranging
honks and roars of dinosaurs and saber-toothed
tigers, which shivered foliage-freighted oaks to
splinters, grasses seared, and dined with deities
upon the flesh of
rams and goats.

Millennia afterwards, Theseus[22] was sighted sky-striding,
eclipsing Helios'[23] pyroclastic car, shuddering and
traversing that bright upper air, bronze armor
corroded, with loosened limbs and ligaments,
yet still maned
and roaring.

Dinosaur and sabered tiger have long-since been
extinguished,

---

[22] Thesus: The legendary Athenian hero who killed the
Minotaur in the Labyrinth of the Minoan palace on the island
of Crete.
[23] Helios: A Greek god of the sun.

driven over cliffs to massive freeze-framed deaths,
then drifted in near-disanimation, like tinted fog,
into the shadowed halls of Hades.[24]

Saber-toothed ourselves now, we have no further
need of
heroes or their eruptions, encapsulate in bronze
equipage. We may take a blotter to the sun, and
congratulate ourselves on our pyrrhic, and
ephemeral, dignities.

1-18-09

---

[24] Hades: An ancient Greek name for the Lord of the
Underworld, sometimes identified with the chthonic aspect
of Zeus and/or Dionysus

Glimpses

Hidden lands lie occulted behind each quantum
particle
we have identified, dark side of every
atom turned toward the light of our inspection,
within
those un-noticed openings between the
things which we have cognized —
sunlight, chickadees, rocks, leaves, lips,
eyes with their reflections —
and, if glimpsed, they shoot away in stages, leaving
fragments
of dimensions in their wake, universes
reeling wave-like in
infinite regression,
like the instantaneous disappearance of barnacles
within
their shells, and we are left to wonder as we gaze
upon the surface of the world
we know as certain:
What else is in there? Could I stand in other places?
Could I
breathe? Would these be habitable if I were
quick enough to seize them?

3-24-13

Whales, Chimps, Hands, and Trees

Whales are wolves of immense proportion,
disguised
as fish. Chimps are human beings pretending to be
apes.

Bathtub drains and galaxies go round and round.
Branching trees, river deltas, frost on window
panes,

palms of your hands — there are, say what you
wish,
hidden patterns upon which everything is
mounted.

And she who sees beneath appearances, though
seldom counted, has touched the face of Deity.

10-19-04

Than We Normally Care to Think

Striated, drizzle-dangling clouds in racing sheets
and tatters scudded
past the undersides of mist-clumped, hypnotic
aggregations,
mounted without warning a grey, half-shrouded
glimpse of
basilicas and mosques from some Otherwhere
behind their watery imitations,
and reminded me that Elysium is weirdly nearer
than we normally care to think.

2-28-16

Breakthrough!

Going along, going along, going along…
Wait! Wow!!

Wha…what the hell was that?!
That! That!

Can't you see it?!
You can't??

Wha…?
Well now, there, it's gone.

……………

I don't know what that was.

9-19-15

Hallowed, Hushed Yearning

Who is that young summer woman with the sky-
blue eyes,
puffs and concentric creases around them, as if she
were aged,
yet with the face of a girl, cream-colored skin,
blonde as sun
on bleached corn tassel?
Who is that girl at our screen door, wanting to take
my hand —
not smiling exactly, yet certainly not unpleasant,
who wishes to walk with me across the fields to the
"University,"
so that I can further my "education"?
And who is that in the shadowed back bedroom,
representing
herself as my dead grandmother, lying on her side,
greyish,
like a half-overturned
baleen whale, offering me her money, blessing me
on my way?
I would say both are angels,
or God Herself, appearing to me as these in this
dream. What
I feel is such joy and gratitude, a great weight
lifted, and a hallowed, hushed yearning.

2-18-16

Nature,

Which Is Always More than That

Vistas

Except within a World

Why instead of nothing has a universe been
unfurled?
Because there is no where to meet except within a
world.

3-19-14

Incantation

Enchanted be the trees, hushed to aromatic
greening,
heavy with summer's sleep and bountiful leafage.

Enchanted be all oceans and seas, still as mirrors,
save
spume and flash of dolphin's leap.

Enchanted be all grasses, herbs and weeds, offering
delicate
humidities to afternoon heat.

Enchanted be all animals with feathers, fur, or
scales,
enchanted be all creatures of the unlit deep.

Enchanted be all planets and stars, all moons and
vagrant
gasses, all things bitter and all things sweet.

Enchanted be all lakes and streams, all earth, all
rock,
all mountain's stony sweeps.

Enchanted be all clouds, all gusts, winds and
breezes,
enchanted be the lightning's streak.

Enchanted be the human species, all angels,
demigods
and demons, all light and darkness, and all deities.

Enchanted be all things that have already passed,
all things that are or ever will be —

enchanted by Love that knows no cease, Bearer of
Mildness, Bringer of Peace.

Enchanted by Love let all things be.

2-2-12

The Wind in the Leaves

You say it's only the wind in the leaves.
I say, it's God whispering through these.

You say it's only birds singing.
I say, you haven't heard the real meaning.

You say it's all by chance.
I say, chance is a form of destiny.

You say I'm imagining things.
I say, you're the one doing the imagining.

You say I'm dreaming.
I say, it's you who's fallen asleep.

3-3-15

This Will Not Be Said!

This august, breathed enthrallment, this layered
thundering, tiering, pounding, wasp to larva

hammered incorruption, chiseled utterance, brick
to brush, this felled stillness, risen thrustment,

unto which, or as, arrive-and-vanish timber, stone,
ice and fire, between these panting flashes,

shouting, dancing, continuance unto cadavering —
likewise self-exhumed as seed to shoot, branching

leaves of iron, furrowed brows, cragged stare or
gaze, crashing through this verdure. I know what
must be tranced

and manifested here, at every locus, yet I cannot
speak it, wrestle it into being, or adequately
imagine it.

It recedes from any language I might speak. This
will not be said, localized, grasped by eye or hand,

gained through intercourse of brain and spirit,
tooled, worked, depicted, or rendered drastically.

Where is there any here or when, still-to-then, then
tumbling from exhilaration to the plundered
canvas?

Sharks, horses, dragonflies, grubs, trees, tachyons,[25]
carnivores and caprids, serpents come unbidden,
panoplied,

everted, self-occuring from some matrix of
fecundity, some exultation of binding brightness
of which I am inescapably
ignorant.

I do not know what manner of thingness is this
whelming — wondrous, awesome, all-portending —

vision or this dreaming, or by what this has been
constituted through awareness of my awakening.

I will be hushed to dust before I know the Sources
of my makings.

8-7-07

---

[25] Tachyons: Sub-atomic particles

Naturing

Can you hear Nature naturing?
Is that a terrible sound, or benevolent?
Is it a clashing of something with nothing,
or is it only mindless data?

I don't know — except that there certainly is
intentionality.
That seems to me quite a bit significant — this,
and what I think is glaringly apparent:

Nature wishes to escape itself to become
fulfilled, and thereby self-transcendent.

7-12-15

The Soul of Nature

If you will go down into that deep and bottomless
well
which is the Soul of Nature, brave enfolding
darkness,
heartbreak, the inconsolability of its certain doom,

if you will entertain its all-enveloping anguish at
incessant
eating and being continuously consumed, you will
grasp
what the apostle Paul wrote vis-à-vis that Gnostic[26]
truth

that Nature, with all Her creatures, groans like a
woman in travail
to give birth to those embodiments of God Who
will raise Her
with their own ascent into some disincarnate
looming,

and deliver Her of Her many-faceted, half-formed
features to that

---

[26] Gnostic: Gnosticism was originally an ancient Greco-Near
Eastern spiritual orientation which taught that the explicated,
or existentiated, world is seriously and irremediably flawed,
and that the human task is to realize this and begin the
process of transcending it. In addition, a reference to the
Apostle Paul's image of Nature yearning for fulfillment in his
Letter to the Romans, chapter 8, verses 18-19

day-light world above. If you chant a psychic song inspired by
Nature's sorrows, one that speaks without self-muting,

crows and ravens assuredly will hear you, and assemble at some
nearby tree, soon more dark than leafy. You will be singing that
to which they are pre-existentially attuned,

and they will keen as well in caws and shrieks along with you,
and know you as a portal to that realm from which they too
have fallen, for which they likewise long,

above the sky which is their cage's roof.

4-7-09

More than Counting Zebra or Gazelle

Nature creates from within, boot-strapping on each creature's
actions into the next available place-and-time — call it an
"adjacent possible."

By this means it demonstrates that it wishes to go somewhere
it hasn't been. In this sense at least, each process within it
is teleological.

Each seeks fulfillment in infinite self-completion. Causality is not
about clacking billiard balls, though mechanical procedures
are evidently permissible.

Randomness isn't that. Or, even if it is, it's still causative, and grist
for Nature's mill, which demonstrates goals, albeit only half
awake and less than keenly —

for example, natural selection. Call it "natural." It's still selection.
Sleep walking has its compulsions and finalities. If serpents
are always dreaming,

they nonetheless stalk and feed. If people behave
unconsciously,
they nevertheless wish well-being. Nature is
directed by
mathematical and geometrical

laws, on which it thrives, and which, whether
precedent or inherent
to it, it is pleased to utilize in its self-elaborating
agenda,

in which each entity is a value in itself, and, at the
same time, vis-à-vis
Nature's program as a whole, variously
expendable.

I don't know where Nature comes from, or where it
thinks it's going.
But consciousness was evolved, I think, for more
than counting
zebra or gazelle.

8-5-12

That Which Isn't Really

The world is a copy of something,
but something that is no thing.

This renders it revelatory and opaque
both to intuition and to intellectual
scheming.

As a copy, it points in the direction
of its original, which nonetheless
cannot ever be singled out or seen.

That is obscured by the teeming nature
of the world, or say, the sheer intensity
of its sheening.

While I do not question its reality, as some
have, I do have my doubts about the
completeness of its being,

which deficit, I think, it tries to rectify
by its ceaseless quest for meaning.

But no matter what it does, a copy can
never be its original. That doesn't
mean it isn't pleasing.

It does, however, indicate that things can never reach the state, as they, as that which isn't really.

10-12-14

Apocalypse

The only end of the world that merits the terms
"eschaton,"[27] "apotheosis,"[28] or "apocalypse"[29]
is what occurs to the spirit when it lifts above
the realms of math and physics
after long discipline or sudden joyous turning,
and finds itself surrounded and swept up
in soundless music
en route to vanishing and reconfiguration in light-
washed fields of previously unimaginable
spaciousness and completion.

12-21-12

---

[27] Eschaton: "The last things"
[28] Apotheosis: Achieving oneness with the Divine
[29] Apocalypse: "Showing forth"—ultimately the full Self-
disclosure of the Divine

That Singular Identity

In death, Nature reaches, not its nadir, but its
zenith, and
lofting up and through its nullification at apogee
in zero, vanishes with relief

into the One Who is No-thing, All, and every one of
these.
What evaporates with sparrow's fall and
dissipation
of the mind streams

forth cornucopic the other side of negation,
tumbles out
into the Light, jostling, cawing, roaring, singing,
fills
uplands of the Pleroma with high hilarity,

and thunders, rainbowed and diaphanous, unto the
very
verge of Deity, or, surging further as a sort of
golden
spume or mist, subsides into its Origin, and,

disrobed of every form, becomes that Singular
Identity.

7-21-13

Creatures

Here Let Them Abide

Standing, feet well-planted on this rough threshold,
fronting the night full-on,
I hold the door wide open, brace it with my left
elbow and forearm
against the outside wall. Beyond the spill of light
from illumination back behind me,
an infinite blackness motionlessly displays. I wait
hopeful, expectantly
for all of them to arrive. For I've called, on Good
Authority, all living things
in from outer darkness. God, make me sufficiently
great-hearted to take them in,

and here let them abide.

5-16-15

Yucatan

I have arrived and known myself alive in the
rainforests
of Veracruz, Yucatan, and Quintana Roo,

and felt like one of Moses' Israelites crossing the
Red Sea
between two interminable walls of water —

only I was driving down a ribbon of asphalt, and
the walls
were green, massed trees and underbrush towering

on either side, nearly closing out the sky. I was
stifled by
humidity, and feeling mildly claustrophobic.

Life! Life! Life! as far as the eye could see, a thick
smell of
minty chlorophyll, of sap, of bark, wet soil, and
rottage.

Here, life was absolutely victorious in its struggle
for the light,
aggressive even, and, if truth be told, a little
ominous.

Exuberant nonetheless. I'd inserted my miniscule
and passing
presence here, felt blessed and awed

by my fellow living things, their triumph, and by
their titanic,
if not wholly human, God.

2-2-16

I Have Been Thrilled

I have been thrilled by the warm, nervous wildness
of the rabbit
which lives under the bush by our basement
backdoor,

by the elegant power of that family of does and a
buck that
delicately nibbles our irises, then, started, bolts and
soars,

by the sweet-grass aroma of the pools at Ein Gedi
above the Dead
Sea, the spirit-felled stillness of dusty Teotihuacan
mornings,

the shellac on the shell of the damselfly's eye, the
wave-like light-
lumbering of fleshy green caterpillars — and many
things more.

In spring I stand tingling at the violet and vetch,
carpeting our
front garden, lushing and nude,

the acrid-sweet sting of rising evergreen sap, the
unfurling of
pinecones, the pulpy explosion

of earth-moving tulips shoving up in slow-motion
from their humus-rich tombs,

wasps zooming and zizzling, trailing spindly
appendages, appearing

frenetically out of the blue — all these and more too
numerous
to name, this profusion of creatures pouring forth
into being.

I am exhilarated, seized by a sense of salvation for
this miraculous
jubilation of the Fountain of things!

In these I see the Limitless sculpted and shaped
into finite existents
in time and space, as if they'd been carved off from
infinity

and dropped into place, yet made of the same
Substance by the One
Who simulates, is Himself each uninterruptedly,

without losing even a mite of His Unity — indeed,
gaining His Own
Self-identity by His joyous creating!

1-30-16

Ghostly to Ecstatic

I have stood on a beach in Miami transfixed by
clouds above the Atlantic,
rising up and blooming in my sight like fantastic
ethereal fungi, inexplicably
appearing upon an elevated glassy sheet or bed of
blue, due, I know, to a process of evaporation
from the sundered deep, invisible the interlude,
then suddenly tumbling magically
as humid, filmy phantoms, like breath condensing
exponentially at high altitudes,
no sign of passage,
molecule by molecule — that vast symphony of
transpositioning water somehow managed —
gravity to spirit, beauty to beauty, joy to joy,
ghostly to ecstatic.

2-22-16

True Paradise

"And that this place may...be thought true paradise,
I have the serpent brought."
                    Twickenham Garden," John Donne

Coming home from a meeting one mid-summer
evening, dusk fallen
in amber curtains and that musty purple-grey of
vineyards fruiting,
rusting and shrouded in mist,

I turned into the walk from my car to my study,
suddenly frozen, stunned,
catastrophically stricken. Before me, to the left of
the stoop and my
portal, barring my entrance

thereto, some black shadow, like a sapling, but
branchless, reared from
the earth unnaturally, held a motionless pose, a
thick-muscled manikin,
dry, silent as death,

yet clearly alive though lightless, up-thrust and
eerie, some eruption from
that subterranean all living creatures must dread —
some para-plutonic
discharge,

congealed and, it seemed, saurocephalic. Shock, a
cold jolt of electricity,
spiked through hair, bone, and marrow, like
lightning to my forebrain,
simultaneously

searing and freezing. I instinctively knew in what
presence I was — plunged
involuntarily into that ancient numbing, sub-
volitional harrowing of all
mammals and avian

creatures when caught in welling proximities to
that which is hairless,
featherless, paw-less, that which maneuvers not by
means of fins,
claws, or hooves, but slews on its belly.

What I saw up-standing four feet or so, raven
trunked, solid but supple,
sleek, muted, listing, jet, holy, hellish, that stiffened
bough, flickered
a forked tongue with wide-slitted lips,

eyes indistinguishable from the massive erect
pillar, but clearly fixed
with more than casual intensity on my study door,
as if watching
and listening, bolt-still, like reptilian

heraldic devices on beached Viking ships, or
Eratosthenes' upright sticks
for measuring Earth's curvature.[30] It seemed
paralyzed, like petrified
wood, its wyrd strangely sculpted like flaking shale
or schist.

This filled the now-light-years-long distance
between me and my entrance,
rendered my reaching it completely unfeasible.
What was he seeing?
To what was he listening? Nothing of vision or
conceivably audible.

I realized with a start he was reading or listening,
perhaps tasting,
vibrations from the patterns of ink on the pages
stacked on my
desk, wherein were inscribed poems in honor of
serpents.

Whatever else his presence might have portended,
he was, I fathomed, an
hierophany of holy and most august Deity, from
that atemporal epoch

---

[30] Eratosthenes (c.276-194 B.C.E.): Ancient Hellenistic Greek
mathematician who measured Earth's curvature by means of
a widely-spaced array of upright sticks

of Nun,[31] before Zeus, Jehovah, or Marduk[32] had
been imagined.

He was unquestionably Nilotic, at least as hoary as
herds of Zebra timelessly
grazing, anterior to *homo hablilis*[33] flaking flints. He
was, most starkly, wholly
other, utterly thus — not-me — made concrete and
indisputable,

a living rod of ebony, embodiment of that very
wand which, magic,
smoking, had eaten the wriggling staves of
Pharaoh's sorcerers,
clogged the river's inundation with blood-colored
silt,

raised plagues of locusts, frogs, slew Egypt's first-
born — when cast
in bronze, universal healing depicted. But he
answered to no
higher god, and was, aboriginally, not at Moses'
bidding.

---

[31] Nun: The ancient Egyptian "God before God," Who was
conceptualized as All-thingness/No-thingness
[32] Marduk: The ancient Babylonian god who slew the Dragon
of pre-creation Chaos, and brought the present world into
being.
[33] Homo habilis: An early hominid, perhaps ancestral to
modern humans

He had taken my study for a shrine, which, in fact,
I had built, word-by
-word, and had called him up from clammy
tunnels beneath the
sod, from woodland tress dripping, from long
grasses hissing,

like magi to a crib—though not for obeisance, but
to partake, imbibe,
feed upon the regard due him, which had been
emitted by that
place. I as well felt valued by his appearance,

for having served, it seemed, a worthy conduit
which might in this way
speak to animals across that immense cleft dividing
my species
from every other, and won by dint of cerebral
massifs

some transient hegemony above Nature. There is, I
thought, right here,
albeit disconcerting, proof of some fabulous
communion, mantle-
like, or the iron core of the Earth, primordially
spinning,

semi-molten, an hieroglyphic oracle or lexicon,
deeper than discursive
modes of thinking, wherein all communicate,
mutual and

homoousian.[34] Yet something had to be
accomplished,

some act of irreverence undoubtedly, if I were ever
to reach my door
and the safety, however impermanent, of my office.
There was no
question I was afraid of him — this netherwordly
configuration,

this up-shot geyser of my own self-negating, which
I'd inadvertently
conjured and quickened to life, this outbreak of that
which
constitutes the so-called "imaginal"...and isn't.

Even when I unreeled the hose, and turned on the
water, he stirred not,
nor noticed. So I washed him — aimed for the head
and the ash-black
flank. He ducked, bolted, all seven or eight feet of
him,

disappeared into the brush. With his leaving — I
knew, irreversible — I
immediately succumbed to heart-compressing
regret at the passing
forever of our confabulation, my flush of fear,
anger, and malice.

---

[34] Homoousian: Greek for "the same substance"

I had invited *him* with my words of hallowing, of veneration for his
species, then ignominiously dismissed him when he'd felt esteemed
by my call for adulation. I was ashamed for the terror I'd felt
at his epiphany,

which I'd asked for, and my betrayal of him via the instinctual parabola
of my primate revulsions. Like all concretized entities in this world
of enmity and predation, we'd had to diverge, blessed and
cursed by our ineluctable declensions.

Still, beyond all "this's" and "that's," we'd had our uncomfortable
union. I'd had a moment to worship and wonder. He'd gifted
me with that. I'd gifted him with my words to his credit.

And, in that Egyptian Sekhet Aaru,[35] so I believe, he and I, rhinoceros,
crocodile, wren, whale, and kudu will know ourselves both
multitudinous and one. I hope that he, by now

---

[35] Sekhet Aaru: One version of the ancient Egyptian Afterlife

already
a soul transfigured,

gone before me into that land of smothering
darkness and exaltations
of light, this very moment overlooks my
discomfiture when we first
met in the flesh on that dusk of our planet's
inveterate ambiguity, forgives me,

and will return my proffered friendship, however
disfigured I then
rendered it—this, when I'm white and naked in his
Kingdom of Dis.[36]

8-10-09

---

[36] Dis: Another name for the Greek god of the Underworld

Cows

In the bitter-sweet, rough-tufted grass, in the shade
of this and that dark-verdured tree,
stood they, statued, still-life-hided, rooted to the
earth,
unwilling or unable to shift their mass,
stamp stony legs, hooves-and-feet,
or, rippling, twitch
shaggy casings, mirage-like in mid-summer heat.

Nor did some angel, billowing robes of light,
descend upon that field
from the smoldering blue above the trees to preach
to them salvation.
Death would be their only fate — death in the field,
in the barn, or in the slaughter house,
as yet undreamed.
Indeed, by that self-same misfortune they would be
finally freed.

Thus cows, as well as all creation, will be lifted by
whatsoever means,
however gentle or extreme,
into apotheosis with the One Who once
imagined them.

10-27-14

The Bird

You realize, of course, the bird that perches on this
Maple bough,
far from decoration for the human ear — closer
perhaps to praise

of the sun, his resplendent and brutal lord — is
actually howling.
It is a dinosaur sound, and takes no cognizance of
human
hermeneutics.[37]

The voice is deceptively musical, due to the
diminutive measure of
pipes and lungs. It cries, "Me! Me! The rest of you
are food and refuse!"

9-10-05

---

[37] Hermeneutics: Principles and practices of interpretation,
particularly of a text

Swallows

The boy I was at four or five witnessed what he
took to be
the vast loneliness of swallows as they darted,
swept,
coruscated, glided,

then seemed to languish mid-air, beyond his reach
to sing
or comfort them, waffling in a hollow, sharp-
winded
November sky.

His flesh chilled to frost-indicted marrow at that
sadness
of Nature he imagined, passing, passing, passing
into extinguishment

without love or consolation, each bird dancing,
acrobatic
yet alone in that biting space of grey. He foresaw
their isolated dying.

But he found a cure, pictured to himself, and felt
within and
everywhere, some Deity of Love Who lifts all this,
transfigured as it falls,

into a realm in which Nature's longings are
fulfilled, behind
and higher than mindless skies and ruined tombs.

There predation and defense no longer constitute
necessities.
Well-being is sufficient. The Venus flytrap rests at
peace
beside the bristled fly.

There is no pain or death, and loneliness is merely
an antechamber
to being born again through a gentler and more
loving
Womb.

8-4-09

This Tree

What largely voiceless blows have shuddered
through the fretted
grillwork of this precipitate tree, or any other
entity — the meat,

the pith of it, or any of these, lunging up against
prevailing winds
in order to existentiate, to be made, or make itself,
to be — this,

from that which, on the nearer side, appears as airy
nothingness —
some innate, if ill-defined, potential — yet when
cognized from
within the realm of matter, bespeaks frank
substantiality?

What buffeting of becoming has battered at and
gnarled, bark-
stripped, and twisted this into its present shape —
one concedes,

these most aptly realized epiphanies of forms,
texturing, tinting,
the details of its particular, or their specific,
destinies —

of which potentiality, though held in high esteem
as precedent —

in that sense, unadulterated, impassable, or perfect
authenticity —

nonetheless has proved itself dependent — this, via
the medium of
place and temporality, and broke above it, or up
from underneath,

with little resonance, vaporous streaks of that
primordial fog of
seething protons[38] — mastered by watery
inundations and the igneous?

Still less well-cited ice, gliding stiff and mindless,
continental drifts
and lava, throbbing, chthonic, faults of rock,
fractals of familiar
existence —

involuted with the roots, freezing by turns,
choking, burning,
snapping these, assaulting all at once or
incrementally — the
frosts of equinox and solstice heat —

trunk, branches, flowers, fruit toward this ever-
highing vanishment,
yet at the same time wrought this wondrous thaw
or freshening —

---

[38] Protons: Sub-atomic particles

the notion of the thing itself, or any other thing,
pristine, inviolable, yet
fragmentarily realized, fractured yet up-standing
from that background
blankness

from which this unrecallable ipseity[39] arose or
became invested — embodying
not fully tree-transcending Tree-ness of Edens of
vast solidity, rather
an instance of the series,

concretized, bodied-forth and equally concealed,
yet in this very tree
completed, glorifying substantiated archetypes,
and thereby making
its Envisioner here-and-now, and incontestably
real.

1-17-05

---

[39] Ipseity: The inner and hidden essence or "thingness" of an
object of perception

Cumuli

(Inspired by the opening lines of Wordsworth's "To the Clouds")

Bone-white cumuli suddenly materialize from
behind that unrespiring massif,
mass, manifest, and rush across the startled
underside of dazzling blue,
instinctively retracting,
like a flight of ectoplasmic[40] residue suddenly
released from some deeper sky
I cannot see, nor wish to,
spill across my vision in lumps and smudges,
bleached, eerie, eschatological.

1-13-15

---

[40] Ectoplasm: A ghostly substance

Gravel

Slung gravel clatters dryly, then lies utterly
inanimate,
extra-biotic, dead-as-ever, and of no further
interest.

Bone lies in heaps and piles, silent as the carved
cave's darkness,
post-biotic, psyche ceased, and of enormous
interest...

to psyche, which significance gravel entirely
misses, being
devoid of consciousness, and thereby
unremittingly senseless.

9-17-15

Everything Is Alive!

If, as David Chalmers[41] opines, there is "something it is like"
to be a thermostat,
and that even in the vicinity of electrons[42] is Mind,
then perhaps
my dismissing of gravel
above was at least a little short-sighted, and maybe unkind.
In fact,
my own suspicions about Psyche and Dr. Chalmers' closely
align. So, I'm glad
to unravel my "illumination" about gravel, and suggest that
everything, in a sense, is alive!

1-30-16

---

[41] David Chalmers: A contemporary philosopher of mind who views subjective experience and identity as irreducible to matter, and who proposes that all material objects and systems may be accompanied by a mental, or psychic, component
[42] Electrons: Sub-atomic particles with positive charge

Selene[43]

O moon, moon mellifluously singing, all-alluring
siren,
thou art enchanting, thyself enchanted. Thou art
inaudible,
yet heard reverberating through the ringing core
of us,

eternity aspiring, where light meets Light, and all
are
smelted to an incontestable thinning. Transmitting
night's illimitable
hollow, thou standest watch between sky's roofless
slippage
into nothingness, which is our greatest fear,
dispersion
from mortality to zero. O moon, thou glidest in the
midst of this,
rescuing and soothing.

You neon portal, narrowing to a shiver, wafting
vacuum
back, you make fair entrance for us. Inscribed
upon thy fantastic
limen, uprights, and thy lintel,

---

[43] Selene: An ancient Greek name for the goddess of the
Moon

you mark our way from fragility to endurance,
salvation
indicate, and, past thy gate, draw us by thy
quake and withering
unto oneness with the Deity.

2-13-09

I'm Not Speaking about the World

You know, I'm not speaking about the world as it
is.
It has no future in the direction that it's heading.

I'm talking about what lies beyond it, within it
even now —
this, in a totally non-linear sense.

I'm talking about its disappearance into a supra-
natural dimension.

I'm talking about its sublimation. I'm speaking
about
its destined end in vertical fulfillment.

7-16-15

Seasons

March Dawn

Dawn launches from the south-east through
backyard trees,
verging the undergrowth, cathedraling our lawn.
Long-drawn extruded wash of white, it crashes
soundless
past buds, articulating leaves
like a super-celestial wave hurled landward from
over-brimming seas,
and breaks against our painted walls, laving our
interiors,
strikes fire to all things that it reaches
in a blaze of gold and orange, pastel blues, flashes
of red,
immolating greens,
and bursts in pinks over the plastered halls,
transubstantiates
these into a state of awe,
decants and brings to view that land of dreams,
Elysium,
ever-sought, seldom breached,
yet present here and now without disguise or veil,
present
physically, and by such voiceless cry revealed.

3-25-09

Refurbished in Its Entirety!

The feeling was unlooked-for in early April,
unexpected wholly, startling even —

just suddenly there, an impression of vast
sublimity, palpable, serene.

It arrived as a deliverance, an immensity of
relief, in which words, had they been

spoken, would have fallen vaporous from
the air, dissolved, and come to nothing,

or silently slipped into the dampness of the
earth. It inspired in one a light-filled grace,

a green provisioning, loamy, soul-exalting,
some olfactory trace

of nearby kitchens, half-hidden by the trees,
robins singing,

an opalescent atmosphere caressing lungs and
throat, "other" yet interior.

That dark, hard winter, experienced as an eternity,
disappeared in one fell swoop!

The weight of slate-slabbed skies lifted,
transformed into a hazy blue.

Such gratitude, delight, surprise, baffled joy
surpassed, and Paradise, the very thing,

was entered with a single footstep on the grass.
There was a lilting,

a brushing past some scrim or lighter fabric
which one imagined separated

one's breathing from the lack of it. This was
drawn back, and started toward aliveness,

one went striding as if from death to life,
encountered a compelling succulence,

the presentation of the world as new, or the
old version, refurbished in its entirety!

4-13-11

April Meteor

All hail the meteor's stark-white, sudden plummet,
flame-fisted, air-cleaving,
that neon streak, flashing track-to-impact just
behind those night-dark trees
along the street, a momentary blazing, right there!
across the clavicle and the tibia!
It smeared a path past layered glass-and-screen,
that racketless transiting from
stone-cold sleet
to soundless grounding in some black-wrapped
cornfield to the north and east,
some altogether unanticipated meeting of blank
facticity and oracular or enacted
meaning.
What? A sign or symbol of each ruptured out-of-
nothingness coming unto being — these
contiguous and fabulous things,
crackling, fractured, less than quantum math, then
instantaneously concrete!

It's not like that really, but it is so in dreaming —
some miraculous descent from might-be unto
seeming.

12-4-12

Slow Spring

Spring has been extraordinarily slow in coming this year.

Inch-by-inch it's been dragging out from under that arduous white stifling that was last winter.

Sometimes human lives are like that, after disaster, when the attempt is made to shake free

of recalcitrant darkness, some chest-crushing bereavement, an unstaunchable hemorrhaging of tears.

But summer will discover us all at last. It will sun and green us, re-clothe us in lush verdure —

if not in this life, then in some higher, incomparably more resplendent and insuperably replete.

4-26-14

Hedges at 8:30 P.M. on June 8th

Go deep into the dark in-between, into the dusk
that spaces
leaf from leaf and dwells there with insistence,

keeping thing from thing, letting each thing
breathe, be what
it wishes, what it needs, before its time to seem is
finished.

Go deeply into that shaded nothingness which
expunges subtly
what might once have connected these, or they
with us,

I with you, before that archaic fall that rumbled
softly, then
incrementally sundered us, after I and you'd been
one.

Delve deeply into twilight herbage, into this
progressive evening
which separates by insinuation smooth and fluted
edges,

which whispers, "This far, no further," sets up
enmity between
buckthorn and viburnum, coyote, shrew, and
insect.

I say, go deeply into that velvet midnight which
abides between
those interstices through which you've lately been
reputed.

In there is the Land of the Forever-dead, from
which these visibly issued,
into which they are diminished, from which you
yourself obtruded,

into which you also will be quieted, none of you
excluded. Just peek
now into these hedges. You will not return to your
illusions.

No word will you send back, not a sound. Just fold
into these now.
Feel yourself misting. Now you are less than
aether.

Now you see that you have never been, there
wasn't ever enmity
or distinctness, and, throughout these long-drawn
eons,

you were never even thought of, in essence or
existence.

6-9-14

July Morning

That sharp-white glinting disk of ladled flame
which fires such
life-enticing and astringent effluence between the
dewed and shaded leaves,

abashes all opacities, consumes all fetidness of
black-and-damp,
and sets in motion dancing on this amazed and
waiting morning air.

I salute you at your piped and taloned rising — as
well, He Who
makes you as a sign of That Which thrives in
ceaseless rapture

beyond-above this out-flung roiling massiveness of
outcry, crash, and clatter!

7-28-09

Generations of the Birds

Luxuriantly recumbent, I, in our tree-slung
hammock,
under enchantment of the sun, the whole scene
drafted, I suspect, by Maxfield Parrish[44] —

this, without benefit of *parousia* or the *eschaton*. Yet
nonetheless,
Thy Kingdom come upon our back yard, capacious
as a park, golden and transfigured.

Secured by walls and hedges, drowsing cicada
choirs amply
serenade the orifices of audition with pulsed
crescendos, consensus of releases, then begin again.

Above, in layered leafage, arranged as strata,
appliquéd, finely
drawn and painted, evoking botanical illustrations,
intricate, precise, breathe insubstantial

gusts of light in stately dances, like Etruscan lords
and ladies
on tomb walls, wrapped in netherworldly fogs and
drizzles. Humid shadows glance, Minoan yellows
stir among

---

[44] Maxfield Parrish (1870-1966): An artist famous for what
might be termed the "imaginal realism" of his paintings, in
which the quality of light he incorporates can be described as
in some significant sense "otherworldly"

shades of Roman greens, vaporous exhalations
from heated
stems and leaves, biting, sweet, bunched, alive and
livid vegetation,

breeze-bowed branches, a vague fluttering of
kaleidoscopic
hide-and-seeks, blue sky billowing intermittently,
half-sleeping but auspicious.

I am immersed in this, awash, and by such
redolence conveyed
to sensations of self-dissolving, becoming this
liquidity of flowing trees, a mere whisper in the
foliage.

I am lulled and bathed, drifting near the edge of
temporality,
and gain membership in these uncountable
generations of the birds, each self-assertive, yet
each an instance

merely of the aggregate idea of the creature —
kingdom, phylum,
class, species — unto oneness with infinity, myself
from all this welter nearly indistinguishable.

However, I am restless, and know this irrepressible
identity, which
will not quite let me fade into the dream, or merge
with All-that-is. Actually, I am grateful

for both of these — that nothingness into which I may disperse —
this to varying degrees — and, to varying degrees as well, retain this prescient subjectivity, I, without surcease.

8-16-09

Dora in the Morning

I have risen, and hushed to silence, stood past
doorframe
of our daughter's pink and joy-appointed chamber,

when she lies in a state of after-dreaming, wrapped
in pillows,
sheets, pleasured between the dark of night and
full awakening,

floorboards glistening toward a flood of light,
impelled by
silent breakers from the sun, accompanied by a
shrill of pipes
and blare of spiraled golden horns!

Helios at the window sash ablaze, bows his
flaming head
and sets one molten knee upon the paving bricks
below,

bears witness with his flashing teeth to Radiance
yet greater,
the beast at beauty's bower, breaks his borrowed
power,
shakes out his flaring hair, and causes *her* to glow!

12-01-07

September 5th or So

September 5th or so arose within a chill, ubiquitous
backlit morning, as if a cheesecloth had been cast
upon the world, or frosted glass.

The sun passed behind this like a wind-sheared
animation, something living and organic, the color
of peeled melon or a burnished gourd, gelatinous,

then slibbered down that chrysolite toward
afternoon and evening. The sky cleared to
cloudless, swept and buffed, with neither height
nor depth nor limit.

That came to stand motionless within the trackless
blue of autumn unto which this cacophonous
multitude of things was irreparably receding.

Wasps and yellow-jackets, for all their bluster,
found themselves under sentence of mortality;
leaves once voluptuous now succumbed to gravity.

Cricket legions chanted high-pitched pleas for love.
That completed, their stringy shanks upended.
Frogs prepared for frost and stiffening.

It all seemed almost joyful in its subsiding,
contented even, as it turned toward that dreamless
sleep in which it had been beingless before
its natal stirring.

9-5-09

When the Darkness Came

When the darkness came down round us almost in
an instant,
lowering on apocalyptic clouds, like those
pressurized sulfuric
acid atmospheres of that hell-hole planet Venus,

and slid across the sky out of the north-west,
resembling upside-
down subterranean whales breaching sluggish
heaves of some
doom-impending, inverted sea,

we gaped, astounded and strangely thrilled, along
with several
of our neighbors, then ran for shelter toward the
wreckage of our
home, just that moment stricken from the grid.

In the charged, tumultuous air, limbs of massive,
long-lived
trees splintered, thundered against the roof like
clubs of giants,
and drove into the quaking ground like Titans'[45]
spears,

---

[45] Titans: In ancient Greek mythology, embodiments of the
brute forces of Nature before their defeat by the Olympian
gods

accomplishing such fantastic trans-sectionings and
high wild arcs
in that bone-concussing wind that it seemed the
Earth itself was
both erupting and imploding.

And when that maniacal display moved south and
east, and our
destruction locally was complete, we slumped
down in that blasted,
helpless house. If not precisely homeless,
we nonetheless were refugees.

I sat staggered, not embittered, not feeling overly
impressed by
Nature nor its thuggish mindlessness, nor
passive—rather,
chastened by consciousness of the fragility
which is our civilization—

infra-structures and battlements erected by our
will-to-live, and also
by our hope—I call it knowledge—that we are
other than the
maelstrom, and, in spirit or imagination,
do not share its fate.

9-6-14

Silent Lightning

Some distance to the north last night,
silent lightning between the clouds —
soft illuminations,

then blinding flashes, silhouetted cumuli,
instantaneous, immolating, then otherworldly translucence,

as if Spirit had burst forth suddenly amid
the towering forms of matter, Godhead
disclosed Itself,

then immediately re-cloaked, smoked
and sizzled between those looming
shapes of vapor,

stupefied now and trembling before such
violent displays of preternatural
Ferocity.

7-23-14

Into Our Pasts

I don't remember the exact day the last
cicada rasped its final gasp.
It was sometime in October. Without my
noticing, the summer of our love
had become unrecoverable, and vanished
utterly into our pasts.

10-10-15

The Liquid Slide of Day's Last Light

In the liquid slide of day's last light upon
the pumpkin-orange of our north wall,

I witness life-in-dying, the richness I have
lived, and all of time and space in thrall!

1-30-15

The World Is Old

An almost audible music slides liquidly around me
in the antique light of November,

at times as if I were slipping into a bath of rich
Italian gold.

At other times, it thrashes past and through me like
Beethoven's Ninth Symphony at climax,

threshing shriveled leaves, unprotesting like the
dead. The effect is otherworldly — the stifling,
opaque adagio of the amber, the trumpet blasts

of gold which unfold the air and drive it with its
load of life-shorn vegetation in solid sheets or
disarticulating whirlwinds. It reminds me that

the world is old.

11-24-13

Fine Snow

Fine snow is sifting down tonight, a softly ominous
ground-ward
floating between the naked trees,
the grey-above hung low and featureless. There is
no hint of breeze.
The piling white fills in the paths of squirrels that
earlier bounded
to and from the feeder.
I take it that all animal life is sheltering and asleep.

Would that I were sleeping too. I've had another
nightmarish dream.

Still, if I hadn't gotten up, I would not have seen
this deadly screening
of the world in frozen fog, nor felt its eerie peace.

2-5-14

Winter Apparitions

Winter Sun

This great sphere of wind-blown flame which rises eerily
through leaf-shorn trees on sub-zero mornings,
and passes across that crystalline ocean far above us like a
ghost behind an icy veil, self-absorbed or on an errand we cannot fathom,
cools to a glowing ember as day draws down, casts its dying
red like blood upon the landscape, and falls in silent
thunder behind the border of the world.

Winter Moon

And in its place the moon glides up through those same or
other rimed and glading trees, quiet as the sleep of death, a phantasmal, tarnished mirror.
Seems, and is, portentous. Just below its pillowing luster it
discloses what when shadowed is concealed: deep unholiness, terror deeper still — that stone-cold

heartlessness of the massively inanimate, brutality
of such
stark matter that not the possibility of thought
becomes
occasioned, and tears are less than unconsidered.

Winter Stars

If I cry aloud to winter stars, they do not hear me.
They have no feelings, and are unaware
of the mass and gravity that make them possible
and rule them with an iron rod.
They are, of course, indispensible to my being,
while I am infinitely beyond the capacity
of their caring,
which does not exist in any sense, as they burn
and hurtle, mere expressions of geometry, in
their swarms and their pods.
I resent their violence and stupidity, and do not
consider it a privilege to observe them. Quite
the contrary.
At the same time, I'm glad they are such morons.
I'm too precious to be ogled by a clod.

Winter Night

Sun, moon, stars, all overhead together at
midnight,
and there beneath an olive tree
a Minoan goddess[46] seated bare-breasted in
flounced skirt,
snakes lithe and leaning
about her neck, shoulders, and down her arms
out-stretched.
She grasps them by the nape and stares
at me with eyes
thrown wide, burning alive, a look neither of
benevolence nor glaring,
as if, like a thing of Nature or beyond it, she
barely sees me,
or sees right through.
The tree and she are suffused with a shedding
amber,

aurelian, or reddish radiance, a scene transposed
from some
above-time Mediterranean,
ever-living, about it an ambience

of grotto or cave, forest, orchard, or rock-strewn
plain,

---

[46] Minoan goddess: A number of extraordinary statuettes of
this goddess, probably called Potnia by the ancient Minoans
of Crete, exist.

a sanctuary of life down deep
at the Fundament where fire and blood are the
same,
appearing here
this white winter night
in our back yard, set down in the snow before me —
I,
caught between fascination and flight.
The snow, the un-leaved trees, the frozen sky, its
glinting spheres,
though she has summoned them,
do not interact
with her hierophany, nor she with these. I have
never
seen life and death so dramatically
displayed, so obviously right for each other, and
likewise
mutually intractable.

12-9-13

Ice

The effect of ice, whether intentionally inflicted or ostensibly
meaningless, is to deprive a living thing
of the substance it is made of and which it most desperately
needs to utilize.
Ice means the cancellation of a living being, the freezing,
suffocation, or paralysis of this.
Yet might not such surface silencing signal something more
consequential, perhaps itself alive
within the ice, some breathless Beauty merely half-suspected
previously, and because suspected
feared, now, hair prickling, revealed as full-stop of superficial
life and a freeing of what was deeper?
That is harrowing to find, even if you're looking. What's more,
you have to die in order to encounter it
in its Fullness. But if you stand very still before your bathroom
cabinet, and do not blink,
you will see it watching you from just above the sink.

3-16-14

And It Begins Again

Flowers inundate, in torrents swell, rush upon the
lattice,
delve there toward some climactic gladdening,
bower
now, their circumference blazing

by means of that life-infusing nuclear disk of
midday flame.
Bees, sashed in yellow and black, thrum on tinseled
wings,
furnaced air congealing.

Dusk-thrust, undammed arbors weighted with
massive
fruit, these half-smothered by livening vines, laden
also are
with copper-green and jet-striped snakes.

Stone and soil tend toward celebration, as do all cry
out
to Earth with fructifying jubilation. Ardent Helios
catapults,
over-leaping Hades, his proper zenith gaining,

aether-cloaked and waiting. Night lets fall
prestigious
tapestries, vermillion-tinctured veils. Liquefying
vernal days
expand to eons, bitumined, heated, ringing.

From meadowed hill tops bawl fog-horning
bucephalic
Ba'als. Sea-foamed sapphire heavens split, and reel
with all
that is toward Nature's ancient raising.

Delirious, I clatter at Heaven's Gate, hail-white.
Beyond are
tessellated halls and paving. In all my strivings,
God
has won this day for me and all of these, and
for all of these, ebullience and salvation!

12-10-08

Human Beings

What Is the Human Being?

What is the human being really, that it has
such shadows of magnitude within,
that it projects Soul, Spirit, and very Deity
from deep in its interior onto cosmic
fastnesses, and touches with its furthest
reach Infinity?

10-19-15

The First "Adam" and "Eve"

The cylinder seal[47] rolled out across the clay,
astonishingly,
reveals

"Adam" and "Eve" in "Eden" as they first were,
before the
biblical author altered their story

from one of great good fortune to merciless
calamity, and
thereby changed their fates from ecstasy and
elation
to unremitting misery.

The seal's impression does not depict a fully
unfolded narration.

But it does display the crucial scene — the sharing of
communion-
inducing fruit from the sacred Tree.

Here they are, raised upon the clay on either side of
a wildly
fertile date palm, seated

---

[47] Cylinder seal: Cylinder seals served as signatures in ancient Mesopotamia. The cylinder seal described here has not been precisely dated, but is almost certainly from the 3rd millennium B.C.E.

164

on block-like thrones, facing one another in
attitudes of grace
and dignity,

gesturing to each other with outstretched arms and
open
hands, mutually invitational,

that each might partake of the pendulous, out-
thrust clusters.
The two figures are wrapped in close-fitting regal

garments, poofy skirts below the knees. She has her
hair
in a species

of bun. He wears what looks like an over-turned
kettle with
horns. On their feet are pointy-toed boots or shoes
with high heels.

Significantly, a wavering snake, elevated on the tip
of its tail,
stands guard behind "Eve."

It is pressed close to her back, its head rearing
protectively
above her coiffure. It's clearly her animal
hierophany.

"Adam" and "Eve," Garden, Serpent, Tree.
According to
scholars, the latter of these doubly

represents supra-cosmic Knowledge and
Immortality, twin
characteristics of highest Deity.

Indeed, this is the Garden of the Gods. This first
"Adam," the
king-warrior, and Snake-manifesting "Eve" are two
such salutary beings.

As Mesopotamian myths stand, the Holy Couple is
not at the
inception of our earthly ancestry.

Still, they are in human form. Might we not then
claim them as
indicative at least of our deepest and most
primordial identities?

If so, that aspect of us has always been present
within, and
only needs us to free it.

After all, the first "Adam" and "Eve," like their
blight-and-blasted
revisions, are something we ourselves have
dreamed,

projected out and backward. What we dream is, irreducibly,
of human provenance, and has no other source of meaning.

I stand with Greeks and mystics: both versions of the myth
are true to the Psyche:

in essence, we are cosmic visionaries and eternal;
in existence,
we have fallen out with Eden.

Since our over-riding task is to re-achieve the state
of our rightful
supra-celestial divinity,

I note the tragedy of our expulsion from the Garden, yet hope for
our return to that Date Palm of our noblest self-exceeding reveries.

12-16-15

Our Yearned-for Savior

Adam fell from oneness with the Deity, and, Bang!
the universe broke forth!
He named all creatures as He imagined them,
made the serpent,
and through that sorting
began the long ascent to consciousness. That's why
His universe,
specifically, is anthropic. We are His particularities,
stunned as well.
His Alter-Self, called God-the-Son, while we were
sophomoric,
made the journey down more gently, took the mind
of Jesus,
and became our yearned-for Savior.

10-9-15

Penelope and Odysseus

What a warrior was Penelope,[48] besieged, driven
toward disaster,
striving through a cataract of tears, with force of
mind and soul of iron,

to hold the space of hearth and heart for her strong
and canny
husband, battling, waves away, to be once more
beside her

and live the vision of their wedding day, by twenty
years and half a
world catastrophically sundered, his craftiness no
match for Circe's guile,

his pride defeated by Poseidon's wrath, yet his love
for her, hers
for him, not diminished or retracted — more
effectual, in fact,

than all the powers of Heaven, great and small
together.

---

[48] Penelope: The wife of Odysseus, the Greek hero whose
return voyage from the Trojan War is recounted by Homer in
his epic poem "The Odyssey." Penelope was faithful to
Odysseus in the face of many aggressive suitors for the ten
years duration of the Trojan War and the additional ten years
it took Odysseus to make his way home to her on the island
of Ithaca.

He strove to reach his home.
She strove to keep it that.

Athena, of ivory limbs, attired in black, with ashen-
green and
piercing glance, in heart-felt love for such
exemplars of human
fidelity and passion,

worked without relenting, by phantoms, dreams,
and sudden
inspirations, to reunite the riven family.

Odysseus said to Athena, "Stand by me, Goddess."
Athena answered, "I am here."

And when the bloodbath in the hall was finished,
and wife and
husband had had their reconciling fight about the
bed,

their son Telemachus had become a man, all
Ithaca's[49] affairs
had been resolved and peace restored, they settled
into each other's arms,
and began again.

---

[49] Ithaca: The island home of Odysseus, just west of the Greek
mainland

Their journey had something other than a happy ending.
But perhaps that's not their true significance.

Perhaps our journeys are contexts merely, opportunities
in narrative form for our unfolding,

for moments in which, as we are cast, we reach our heights
and depths, may live our authenticities,

resonate with the realm of spirit, climax, become fixed
realities, reference points, legends, archetypes perhaps,

entablatured above our struggles with each other and our
deities, sans flesh, refashioned into images of historians

and That Which gave us birth — in that refashioning,
rendered immortal.

Who knows?

Whatever of Odysseus, Penelope, Telemachus, or Ithaca there
was, they *are* as Homer told them — and also, I propose, as

they really were, whatever that may or may not have been.
Actually, I agree "we are such stuff as dreams are made on,"

and add that dreams are far more durable than chemistry or atoms.

3-24-12

Side-by-Side

The sun, the moon, the stars, this whole universe in
all its
mystery and magnificence,
when set side-by-side with a single act of human
love, is
suddenly recognized to shrink
to insignificance.
Lumbering brachiosaurs, nebulae, black holes,
quasars,
creaking forests bent low
by hurricanes, and all that astounding resilience
of life
surviving cosmic adversities
or not, is only background and occasion for the
startling
apparition of self-eliding kindness,
which is the core and very substance of whatever
might be
regarded as a bodying forth
of meaning. And when a loved one dies,
everything
that wasn't her or him is known
to be incommensurate with grief — absolutely, and
with finality.

My guess is Heaven itself means nothing for a time
to those
who've undergone that rending relocation.

11-1-13

From Psychology to Our Most Authentic Biding

It is a fool's errand to try to integrate the mindless
brutality
of Nature with what is most human about us.
Oh, we need to do what we can within our
microscopic
faunic designations—reptile, rodent, ape-and-
more—
which have been mounted by it.

There are, undoubtedly, treasures in our muck and
mire, and
we shouldn't be ungrateful.
We should make friends with our animal selves,
sincerely, as
much as we are able.

Why? Because it's where we came from, and where
a part of
us will remain until the dust blows up to claim it.

Also—the real point—because only when there's
relative
stability in the lower dimensions of the psyche
can the spirit,

which is the best of us, be freed to climb into the
Light,
the Homeland of our most authentic biding.

2-22-15

Indifferent Hostility

For all the times I've risen upon you in the guise of
Nature,
and manifested cruelty to your youth and
innocence,
attacked your vulnerabilities,
actualizing for you that shot-through savagery of
death's
mad gaping,
I am regretful at levels and depths of feeling which
elude my
capacities to speak them.

Still, within the Land of Magic, there are ogres and
trolls as
well as angels.
And I am grateful that it was I who introduced
them to you
rather than a stranger's indifferent hostility.

8-17-15

Unforeseeably More Kind

At the confluence or mutual presentation of our
anticipations and anxieties,
where questions can no longer be intellectualized,
referenced as discursive or neutralized
by buffering layers of self-removal or detachment, I
find the friable
edge of Nature, rumbling out from under me,
betrayal and some proffered enterprise
made immediate, personal, yet anything but
intimate, a style
according to which the day-to-day is rendered
radically estranged, despised
even, or at least without significance. In that
breathless instant there is only "I,"
not even that entirely, or in the form that I have
come to know,
and all I'm for and all I am is do or die —
I collapse with Nature's waste, or leave that heap
and step into some bolt of light
which beckons and will transform me, alter
irreparably my earth-emerged identity,
and turn me into some one, or thing, somehow
recognizable
yet augustly rarified,
of many shapes and colors, enormously more
expansive, and unforeseeably more kind.

6-10-13

Our Early Form

We must come to terms with this: when we step
through
the gates of death we are no longer human.

The human was our early form, prerequisite for
what we
would eventually become.

It was one avenue to Infinity. It seems likely there
are numerous.

7-30-10

Evocative of Tears

Like a great tide, inexorably, this vast universe and
each one of its creatures
heaves and glides toward what we call oblivion,
and is
that, from this vantage point of being.
But when all these things slip over into depthless
shadow,
at the instant of their disappearing, they sing.

The music that they make is inaudible to our
hearing, but
sometimes we can feel it brushing past our skin,
or as a sort of tingling,
hair-raising in its implications, heart-stopping,
evocative of tears.

11-6-11

The Human Spirit

The world is rich and filled with wonders,
but it is not enough for the human spirit.

The earth abounds with an extravagance of beauty,
but it is not enough for the human spirit.

The universe is vast, perhaps beyond imagining,
but it is not vast enough for the human spirit.

The human spirit knows unlimited wonder,
beauty, truth, richness.

That is why the identities we have been granted
here are not enough for the human spirit.

7-20-10

Paul and His Mirror

Paul, when he gazed into that patinaed mirror,[50]
did not see behind him; he saw within.
When he looked, he saw the transfigured human,
all creatures, Nature, climaxed at their
completion, rushing up and disappearing.

3-13-12

---

[50] Adapted from the Christian New Testament, I Corinthians
13:12, a letter of the Apostle Paul to his newly founded
church in the city of Corinth

I Feel Sad. I Feel Scared.

Here I am now, alone, homo sapiens, homo sapiens
sapiens,
my siblings and cousins long since cancelled —

dust and rock now, fossil and bone, whom I out-
competed and/or
helped to their respective, and well-deserved,
erasures,

with whom I shared this planet,

whom I knew from a distance, physiognomical,
morphological,
genetic. How distasteful were they to me, except
occasionally,

when I ravaged their women, if you could even call
them that —

australopithecines, nutcrackers, habilines, homo
erectus —
Denisovans and Neanderthals[51] at the last.

Here I am now in my full arrogance, sole possessor
of this earthen
ball, victor over rival kith-and-kin. Yet somehow,

---

[51] All species of early hominids or hominoids, some of which
may be ancestral, at least in part, to modern humans

now our desperate contests are in the past,

regretful about the loss of that, the times we
shared, missing the
comradeship of bonded, albeit bizarrely different,
spirits.

Of course, I had

to rid myself of them. Their presence — those back-
slung protuberating
flat braincases, grotesquely elongated faces,
unseemly

jaws and teeth — made me think of *myself* as an
animal —

the reddish fuzz they called their hair, the moronic
way they had of
chipping flints, the vacant mastication,

their nearly total lack of foresight, art, record-
keeping and transmission,
the general emptiness of their monstrous heads.

Sooner or later, they'd have cashed

it in. It's true I was complicit, but really never more
than an agent of
biology. They barked at un-thought-through
deities,

showed nothing of what I could have called
authentic spirituality.

I was Abel; they were Cain. I was Jacob; they were
Esau. I was civilized;
they were uncouth. I was chosen; they were trash.

Yet, when they passed, I felt a part of me had also
gone down to extinction —
irremediable, that. A brotherhood and sisterhood

of the valiant,

of questors and champions, had been expunged,
and I was left to crow,
but also to my own devices. I mean that literally.

I feel sad.

I feel scared.

Now, it's just me, the beasts and elements —
plagues, droughts,
diabolically errant asteroids, wormholes for god's
sake,

vacuums.

Where are my vanished sisters and brothers?
Where I know I too will go
for all my cleverness — into the mud, the rocks, the
lava flows,

and cosmic anonymity.

10-1-12

Mr. Madsen

In my boyhood, Mr. Madsen, grey skies and wild
places were
inextricably warped, weft, and loomed:

plipping fish; canoes slipping noiseless over
quicksilver skim;
chill lakes and rivers, mosquitoes, deer, flies, loons.

He taught me how to fish, how to string the
wriggling meat,
surprisingly muscular, onto the hook,

to slit the sharp steel through the gushy, twisting
flesh, break
it out the other side, snag another loop.

If I had the hunter's luck, some subaqueous veneer,
feeling
hunger, incorrectly judging, would strike, become

my captive — would dash, veer, run out the line, I
locking the reel,
then hauling, paying it out, locking, yanking until,

flashing silver, he would flip into the boat,
thudding on the
aluminum. I'd grasp him tightly behind the gills,

pry the hook from the raw-boned jaw, his
breathing labored, as
he vainly fought for freedom.

Then I'd guide his thrust, leap-and-slibber, with a
plop into the
murky, white bucket.

In Mr. Madsen's company, I felt the primordial
triumph of
"Early Man" felling herds of mastodon —

murdering some living thing — some-one? —
registered my first anguished
pangs of fear and guilt at brushing

death against another's skin, insinuating that
apocalypse into its flesh
and brain, administering thus a non-rescindable
cupola.

One slate afternoon, late August or September, the
two of us, grinding
our knees, worked debris of limestone flakes and
layered slabs,

avalanched from the flinty bluffs above, Loud
Thunder State Park, once
an inland sea, now a creeked and graveled canyon.

We were fossil-hunting. I remember the smell of
rock-dust and damp
stone, like old basements and garages — as well, the
echoing vastness.

I hoped for dinosaurs, of course, or even only fish.
What we found were
shells, sea urchins, and oddly articulated calyxes
and jointed shafts.

With Mr. Madsen, however disillusioned, I touched
with that my planet's
ancient past, long ages before humankind had,
perhaps,

even been imagined — an utter nothingness in that
epoch, completely
unpredicted then, a wholly insubstantial lack.

I recall a bitter wind. It was December, I believe, at
Mr. Madsen's house.
It was overcast as always, and vaguely
supernatural in the
parousiaic strangeness of his presence. There were
ice-clogged sub-cumuli,
or whatever they're called — like frozen ash or like

evaporated lead,
suspended from an impenetrable heaven

not far above the shingles or our heads. I was
navigating his rickety,
screened-in porch, muffled in my winter coat, scarf,
woolen cap and gloves, inching

through stacks and stacks, whole mountain ranges,
of old National Geographics —
centuries of these, it seemed. The frigid air, like
congealing

atmospheres on Jupiter or Saturn, was musty, thick
as a wall of frost-rimmed
cloud or solidified fog. In what might have been
millennia, the magazines

had sat in unexcavated heaps, which reeked of
moldy paper and printer's
ink, deployed over some long-forgotten sofa,
smothered tables, and
the floor, like semi-hardened

lava flows — mesas, bluffs, crevasses, entire
topographies of these. I
opened some, became immediately transfixed,
especially by the color prints,

precisely executed, of North Atlantic fish, arranged
in page after page of

columns, species-by-species, in silvers, yellows,
muted tints of

tans, browns, cobalt blues, various shades of gold
and grey, meticulously
represented: scales, gills, head-bones, fins,
luminous, large-pupiled eyes.

I thought, 'The artist really loved these creatures.
He really saw them—
their unearthly beauty, that they are, in fact, the
ghosts of some
anomalous and weirdly wise

divinity of the deep, that desolated wilderness of
salt and swell that,
for fish at least, is functionally interminable. His
psyche uses their ice-

block life to climb up from unconsciousness to this
hardened supra-
stratosphere where Beauty, packed in unthawed
grime glints and glimmers,

gazing out from that eons-slow metabolism of
fishes' eyes to behold
the cosmos as a whole, a gazillion zillion light years
wide, where
nothing stirs and no wind gains admittance.'

I was there, through the ragged screen bracing
ocean spray frontally,

thudding through endless undulations of sluggish,
shifting seas!
The smell of fish, rotten-sweet,

thronged my nostrils. The whole scene electrified
me with its mystery.
I was plugged, stiffly frozen. Yet there was
something awakening in
the marrow, some irradiation

from the bone-cold core of me, more central than
the glacial pace of
gradually thickening blood, pushing back against
my unencumbered numbing.

I felt everything there is for fish — this, and ever
could be.

Mr. Madsen was my stocky, square-faced angel,
patron of the cold and
damp, of all lonely and remorseless places — woods
and wilderness, crags and fissures,

of marshes, tundra, ice and snow, of Arctic seas,
redolent of shark and
walrus, and those voiceless, shivery inhabitants of
the deep, the plethora of fishes —

of all bereft and bare spaces within my spirit.

Whenever I find myself with vertebrae
compressed, shoulders hunched

against the blow, the lowering, the cosmic dark —
without,
within, and feeling fetal,

of no account to Nature — this, disinterested and
remote from that exactly
which makes my humanity a thing of worth and
beauty —

or shunned by that same inhuman wall of
intransigence or of ice in the
garb of hominid society, I think, 'This is a Mr.
Madsen day.'

I sometimes feel his presence even now, a
quickness more than memory,
standing by my side when I drop to desolation and
existential abeyance.

He cannot cure the forlornness of Nature, the
solitary lives of creatures —
quavering, mirror-eyed, the hunger unto death of
polar bears and seals,

the crab's sudden start at the mesmerizing, fatal
light-display of cuttlefish,
nor this endless round in general of predation and
its victims.

But he is there, accompanying all lonely and
abandoned things, a small

lamp in hand, lifted to guide them down mineral-
slicked corridors to a deeper Light—

with them always, and with me.

He is a syllable of the saving Word of the Creator,
uttered from within the teem
of Nature's crimes, its insistent nihilism and
absurdity.

As such, he is contiguous with that Speech of Deity,
agent of That Which
thrives in Love beyond the mindlessness of
electron and
the transience of anatomy.

8-14-09

Three Tasks

We are here as we are, light and shadow.

The first task is to separate the light from the
shadow,
for the most part by urging the former into
prominence,
though sometimes roughly cleaving the one from
the other.

Yet we may not abandon our shadows, and leave
them
to cry alone in corners. We must hold and love the
wild
animal as the inner child, fearful and forlorn, as if it
were

an ally, one step removed from supremacy —
however,
granted her or his rightful renown.

The second task is to grasp ourselves whole, as
Nature is whole,
and to become as authentic to our earthly majesty
as circumstances will allow.

The third task is to grow the Light in such a way
that it
gradually swallows everything we have been and
done,

so that it lifts us up and out of Nature, including our own,

makes us compatible with supernal Goodness and Love,

and into Heaven lofts us.

2-27-13

Transitional Entities

The forces of Nature have fashioned us, one
hundred percent,
every jot of fiber, every tittle of synapse,

every word, every thought, each nuance of feeling,
every programmed interaction,
absolutely everything about us and between us.

But that doesn't mean we weren't intended.

We have been ginned up, layer by layer of
enhanced complexity,
jerry-rigged, innovated, opportunistically

crafted from accidents and their aftermaths,
on a wing and a prayer.

But that doesn't mean we weren't sent for.

Indeed, in its constant striving, Nature has
fashioned us to know
a Beyond-Nature, while still as-and-within-it.

It's not contrary to Nature to seek Super-Nature.
Quite the reverse.
In its desire to rid itself of itself, Nature has dashed
us up
to end its oddly insomniac unconsciousness,

and put paid to its incessancy, neediness,
starvation really,
its compulsive creativity, when what it really wants
is peace,
which is to say, a terminal transformation.

We are vehicles of Nature's self-obliteration.

We, and perhaps others like us, are those long-
wrought transitional
entities by which Nature, in its self-transcendence,
is itself transcended.

From and even as the animal, emerges at its zenith
something altogether
startling, other-worldly, and spectacular.

8-15-11

Where God and You Are All-in-All

When a child asks you, "Why is the sky blue?" she
or he is probably
asking, "How does it come to be that the sky is
blue?"

You might respond with a scientific account,
having to do with
proportions of the various gasses comprising the
atmosphere.

Since I have only a general knowledge of such
matters, my reply
would necessarily be more vague, yet, I hope,
reasonably true

to the facts which I would assume were being
asked about. However,
I might also suspect another question within that
query —

namely, "*Why* is the sky blue?" Indeed, whether or
not that more important
question were being mooted, I would want to
answer that one too.

In fact, it seems to me that lurking beneath all
questions and endeavors,
the latter of which in my view are also ultimately
inquiries,

lies a yearning and a fear. The yearning is for
significance. The fear is
that there isn't any. I would propose to address
such incipient
nihilism at the root

by saying something like, "Why is the sky blue? It
is, so that when people
look up into that luminate expanse, they can feel
vast and free, like peering

at their Higher Selves, at that part of them that has
never left eternity,
with which they will be joyfully reunited, long
years hence or sooner,

in one great leap into the vault, a raptured re-
engagement with light
and wings, and a mounting into spaciousness
where God and you
are All-in-all, and everything comes clear.

5-513

Dora's Self-disclosing

On the one hand, according to the stance of
everyday,
our daughter's stages from blastosphere[52] to the
woman
she is moving to embody and be

at some hypothetical end-point in the future seem
uncontestably
a matter of becoming, of evolution even, a
progressive
series of complexifying changes of identity,

interaction between her genetic blueprints or
propensities
and environments, themselves an ever-shifting
congeries
of stimuli, like the mercurial surface of the sea —

on the other, when viewed from a somewhat
different angle
of vision, or by a trick of light, temporality of
location, a
presence fully visited from some realm of thriving

the further side of death and dreaming, as if the
moon,
like a disk of sunlit water framed by gathered trees,

---

[52] Blastosphere: An early spherical form of the fetus

had instantaneously
surfaced from some non-discursive depth,

and been deposited in our living room, wholly
manifest and
yet just as surely hidden, and her growing up were
more a
shrugging of obscuring veils, step-by-step

than, as psychologists term it, childhood
development,
apocalypse more than evolution, revelation more
than an emergence.

I wonder which it is, or if her apparent coming into
being constitutes,
or is, the disclosure of who she somehow always
was, will be,
beyond-beneath, or at her apex archetypally,
an expression of
her timeless essence, and, equally, vulnerable as
cheeks to tears.

12-11-12

The Center of Reality

Don't be dismayed at your dismantling by Nature's gigantic scale or its indifference.

Each of us is the Center of Reality, and of the cosmos, its circumference.[53]

9-2-12

---

[53] This is a reference to the ancient Egypto-Hellenic Hermetic saying that "God is a Circle Whose Center is everywhere and Whose Circumference is nowhere."

Paeans, Prayers, and Divine
Considerations

Sooner Rather than Later

I wish that I could sing a song of such breath-
arresting beauty, it would enchant the whole
world —

not just the seven billions of its people, but all
living things, and the four forces of Nature.

Then everything, as it caught the melody and
cadence, one thing after another, would feel
suddenly
a just-then-remembered yearning, more powerful
than all its urgency of being, would, in that instant,
repent
the whole of its strivings and its burnings,

and, overcome by bliss, like falling, stuporous, into
the perfumed corollas of lilies, happily evaporate
into an exultant aether.

I can't sing that song. I'm waiting for the One who
is able. May that Voice come soon, soon — sooner
rather than later.

7-10-15

Radiant Incantations

O God of Goodness un-occluded, Who shines in
magnitudes of Light beyond all finite calculations,
no matter how extravagant,

Who beams serenely through the darkness that
envelopes us, transluces that, and thereby makes
this wondrous world by Magic,

I, one of Your enchanted ravishings, salute You
from all I am and yet hope to be, from all I've lived
and will still, with thrill of gratitude and gladness!

I raise a cry of joy that might reverberate
throughout this chimed and ringing cosmos, such
that all these creatures which You've imagined

would startle and, awake to Your Exuberance, join
me in this paean, now and evermore alive through
Your radiant Incantations!

1-23-16

All of Us Who Are Alive!

"Birds fly from their nests, their wings
out-stretched in praise of Thee!"

(From the ancient Egyptian "Hymn to Aton")

All of us who are alive are forms You take, O You
Who escape all categories of our senses and our
reasonings—

jackal's hearing, serpent's taste, vulture's smell,
that tactile sensitivity of octopi, vision of
damselflies and bees—

and yet You feel and reason as us all, each one and
all together. I believe, as well, You are that Presence
manifest

in all green and growing things, and that Your
Awareness dwells within gasses, minerals, star's
surging light and gravity!

You have made Yourself into these millions, given
them Your Reality, the only that there is—this,
without Your Self-diminishing,

and drawn apart from these that they might enjoy
their own aliveness, and You may celebrate the
multiplicity of Your ecstatic Self-otherings!

I lift my hands and voice as if You were above me in some Life beyond the sky, and at the same time feel You rise and throb within me!

You are us, and yet we are Your creatures. Thank You for letting us be Your Self-experiences, and gifting us with Your Freedom!

1-24-16

Jupiter Optimus Maximus

(Adapted from the opening invocation of ancient Roman prayers to the Supreme Being)

O God, Father, Optimum and Maximum, if that is the Name by which You wish us to call You;

O God, Father, Optimum and Maximum, in whatever gender You wish us to envision You;

O God, Father, Optimum and Maximum, Who is all divine entities and forces emanating from and integrated into Your eternal Unity:

Hear our prayers: thus we beseech You!

1-19-16

Day Prayer

God, Who has manifested me out of those
unspecifiable depths
within Your most exalted and intimate vanishment,
abysses which
You encompass and comprise of nothingness and
plentitude,
Who maintains this form which is referred to as "I"
within this
dilated and fear-inducing medium, Who is/is not,
exceeding my
capacities to think or to intuit, Who, with/without
appearing,
reconstitutes beyond that hushed portal, framing
shadow,
whelming and ungainsayable,
through which I shall evaporate en route to You,
make this day,
and all those days through which I pass within
that glamour
of Your becoming, wonder, awe, creation,
intellectual gain,
learning, teaching, humaneness toward all these
things which are,
and toward my fellow human beings. And,
knowing that
You may be imagined as such inconceivably
benevolent

and indomitable a Presence, of what I am and all
that is
and which occurs, keep me persevering,
courageous,
and whether contemplating or taking action,
deploying
this "I" with which You have at once revealed and
cloaked Your Essence,
with grace, with wisdom, and with humility.

8-14-10

Blessing

When it fell to my lot to be crushed,
I looked to You, to Your Eyes,
found welcoming there, and knew that
no expungement from this life
nor extremity of annihilation according to
whatever venue or in any dimension
would ever come to me except by Your
Volition, and that if that should
occur, I would accept it, and know it
as a blessing.

12-7-14

Vicissitudes

You are with me in and as all of these vicissitudes,
sitting or standing, caressing, breathless, side-by-
side with me, adjacent to me, not always felt,
conjured or imagined, in all my moods and
minds—fisting, palming, smoothing, calming,
lifting me.

I respond to all this intimate weather by which You
become occasioned unto me, all such flux and flow,
beyond my power, of matter and my anxieties,
which are ever ending and engendering me.

In contraction, I encounter Your unchartable, of
which I am terrified, which grips my heart, shatters
me to shards and slivers, and that hopefulness dies
by which I had depicted victory, my actualizing of
some climactic self-fulfillment or eucatastrophe.[54]

In expansion, Your very Light ignites, awakens,
and illumines me, and I am cast up like new
continents, shedding oceans in exuberation at my
fresh geography. I soar, light-filled, You-as-me,
drunk completely,

with neither logic nor sobriety, that I might know
Your validation, not unsaid through indifference,
erasure, nor by nullity.

---

[54] Eucatastrophe: A term invented by J.R.R. Tolkien by which
he meant "a sudden joyous turning"

Whether cramped, lost in frigid labyrinths, chilled and shivering by means of Your unspeakable evacuation, or pleasuring in the fullness of Your sensuality, washed by such liberality of solar seas,

You are my Companion, Security, that over-spreading Tree of Life or Vine from which and to which I am in most intimate proximity, stemmed organically, and ever green.

2-23-10

Incendiary

The clockwork, ping-pong lickety-split, methodical
or cloddish
thudding of this stuff, and that stone slab from
which Pegasus[55]
drove clanging hoof, the untransfigured substance
of it,

striking sparks, then thrashed dramatic
muscularity of
leg-and-wing, lifted, scrabbling riven Scalar
Fields,[56] and drove
thitherward into that limitless expanse, clattered
up

and made for mansions without number, palaces
raised by moonlight,
chanted, conjured, layered heavens wherein are
depicted hail,
fiery suns, mirrored halls, all breathed out by ice-
white doves,

and everything plated in electrum. He escaped to
this.[57] But what am

---

[55] Pegasus: In ancient Greek mythology, a miraculous winged
horse
[56] Scalar Fields: Often used in physics to describe the energy
potential of particular forces—e.g., electrical, gravitational,
etc.
[57] Jesus

I to learn when I've burned my conscience in a fire
somebody else
set match to? What am I to gather here, what
become?

Don't I learn, though, to keep my distance, straying
from the course
as it's been proffered, fraying this and every instant
in regions
I can't imagine, but am able to intuit within these
sundered

plasmas, those ravages ensuing of my
morticianing, coins pressed
over sightless eyes, one of these shoved beneath
my tongue to
be spat out on the other side of my come-uppance

at some shady representative of death. Wingless,
hoofless, such
bitterness I feel until it is accomplished, this
bungled meat
marbled, chilled, as if I could continue to feel its
subsidence, and be dumb enough

to love these aggravators of my situation as if they
constituted
messengers of that benevolent Eviscerator Whose
labor is our
misery. Such self-served atrocities do not, I am the
first to utter,

bode well for my salvation. These vaguely psychic
things from which
I turn, burning bushes and the like, indict me, until
I am myself
that unremorseful incendiary, watching the cosmos
come undone,

and every mercenary of horse-faced good and
evil — until, You came
to me with the physiognomy of Plao, Ibn 'Arabi,[58]
Jesus on his
wounded, glowing feet. You drove me out to sea as
if I were
some wave-chasing Phoenician.

When I reached the furthest shore or orbit, and
beached my ghost-
rowed trireme, crowds gathered round me. "What
was your wilderness?"
they asked me. "God," was all I could think of.

6-3-04

---

[58] Muhyi l-Din Ibn al-'Arabi (1165-1240 C.E.): The "Greatest
Shaykh" in theoretical Islamic Sufism. Ibn al-'Arabi's
voluminous writings embody multiple theological and
philosophical points of view, often addressed as what might
be termed an "either/and" approach to the deep questions
about Reality. He can be interpreted as continuing and
complexifying an essentially Neoplatonic world view.

Call It Christ

Call it Christ or whatever you wish: the death is
died until there is no life this side of Mystery.

That crucifixion, however you might conjecture it,
is our human fate, played out along innumerable
trajectories.

Not only ours, every living thing's — the striving
worm alive when it's digested by the bird, the bird
disarticulated by

the cat, the cat halved by the coyote. Not only every
living thing, but absolutely everything there is.

As in Christ all have died, and all that now exists,
has been or ever will be, so in Christ all are made
alive and exalted in Elysium.

4-10-09

Protection

The last way in which God can protect us from
God's Self is by posing as Non-being.
If we were to discover Him in His Infinity, we
would instantly be obliterated, necessarily.
Such love has God for us that He would rather
Himself be nothing than we not be.

7-27-09

A Prayer for Resurrection

We are angels, so to speak, ripping up interstitially,
breaking planes in our ascent through layers of
strings,

bosons, neutrons,[59] and their manifold menageries,
trying to throw off this same-time making and
imprisoning

medium, break free of these darkly dreamed
entanglements, such hyperactive benefactors of
becomings unforeseen,

gain the liberty of our once and future being, and
know ourselves as children of Divinity.

With gratitude for my decanting through Your
geometrized space, Your algebraic teeming, I praise
You, Lord of lambs and lions,

and seek my resurrection, some promised getting
up or rising from this welter of which You
conceived

and formed me, that I might, as ancient Egyptian
sages prophesied, "stride forth like the Lords of
Eternity,"perceiving only Light.

1-15-12

---

[59] Strings, bosons, neutrons: Subatomic structures and
particles

I Remember Your Feelings

I remember standing in our backyard one
summer's night at our old house at 940 21st Street.

I was twelve, thirteen...fourteen, I think, eye on the
looming darkness of the trees,

still-expectant, intensely alive as me against a
fathoming, shoreless sea.

I felt You there in the hint of a breeze,

just there, behind all things that were, had been, or
ever would be. I was almost afraid to breathe.

You asked me if You'd done well. Had You created
a terrible and wonderful beauty?

Was I rapt by Your achievement?

Who were You — my Creator, as I conceived, the
unrecognized artist, my longed-for father?

Or were You some self-resonance from my own
inner deep?

Whoever You were, You were absolutely real. I
don't quite remember the words I felt compelled to
speak.

But I do remember the poignancy of Your feelings.

9-27-12

I've Never Been More than a Heartbeat from You!

I have cast my soul across a boundless expanse of
indigo blue,
like a sigh of dawn or a breath on a mirror
condensing to dew.

I have rushed head-long with stiff-sheaving winds,
and ridden
light quanta through dazzling gloom.

I have throttled toward the zenith where air thins
to a whisper,
then javelined through lava, and at the core
bloomed.

And wherever I've traveled, through hot rock and
vacuum, I've
never been more than a heartbeat from You!

12-12-14

The Voice of God

The Voice of God is less than a whisper.
The jangle of Nature is an imitation of this.
The rustling of Nature gives animation to
the Void,
that blank background before which all of this is
staged.
The drama attempts to reach its climax in
Nothingness,[60]
yet never is quite able.

10-26-10

---

[60] Nothingness: This is a reference to the Neoplatonic notion
that the restless dynamism of the explicated world is due to
its ultimately fruitless attempt to recover its lost wholeness
as All-thingness/No-thingness—the One "above," "below,"
"within," the multiplicity of existentiated entities and forces.

All that Was Ever Present Here

After the grand parade of self-proclaiming entities
has
passed, everything at last is hushed away in
shadow,
and silence falls deeper than the deafness of stone,
you
might think if you were able, but you could not,
"Joy
and sorrow, pleasure and pain, achievement and
failure —
all that was ever present here was God."

2-2-14

If I Could Not Feel the Hand of God

If I could not feel the Hand of God on my shoulder, shaking me awake,

I would know myself lost in a very bad dream, mind-bending and perhaps unabatable.

If I could not sense a Spirit of absolute Benevolence above and with me,

I would fall prey to a cavernous and implacable haunting.

That nightmare would insinuate itself into both flesh and soul, such that I could find no exit from it.

That haunting would reverberate in every fiber of my identity, then possess and swamp me.

These horrors I know, and not as fears only. I have touched them in moments of utmost quaking

when I have felt myself exposed, naked to the demonic, and wholly unclothed of my Deity's making.

12-4-14

Evidence of Higher "I's"

I suspect I'm anchored in some immeasurable
expanse
of time-and-place in which I have been actualized
in
several, or many, half-remembered guises.

There are scenes and scents I know as if
experienced
from within, which do not have the character of
dreams.
Mists part, costumes are exchanged. I am apprised

of certain individuals which I once, or will have
been —
suffered, joyed, lived, died, lived again as "others"
in
different locations, alternative frames of time.

I wonder: Are these roles which I'm playing my
own design —
sets, lighting, stage directions as well? Am I acting
with
such astonishing skill that I am blind

to their self-referential contingency? Are these
lives, and
this I'm living now, creations of this current "I"?
The

answer I receive is unequivocal: I, at least, am not the Writer.

Some other Author, mightier than my present person is
orchestrating all of this. I am being lived, as is the case
for these distant and most intimate identities.

Sometimes when I speak, my voice lowers unaccountably,
rumbles actually in my chest and throat, especially when
one particular ancient, hooded figure, shadows around his eyes,

is present. He is me, or I am he, I think. Yet we are also not
equivalent. When I speak with his voice, I am me and more
than me, yet I am not ventriloquised

or used against my will. Instead, I am merged with quietude —
dense as granite or iron-hard oak — incalculably self-assured.
He is at least as kind and wise

as Plato, Sophocles,[61] Ibn 'Arabi—darker, though,
than flame-
bright angels flaring round the throne of God—
indeed,
eliciting a moonless midnight, like Sylvanus, with
ties

perhaps to that second iterated "I" of greatest
magnitude in
my awareness—he whom I, albeit with significant
caution,
address as "Archelogos,"[62] of proportions titanic,

turbaned, bull horns twined, embroidered, long-
sleeved robe
intricately interwoven with tier upon tier of
explicated
worlds, architectonics of these, and multitudinous
places and climes

without end. I scribe otherwise when he, beyond
the reach of
ego, guides my thoughts and pen, makes
corrections to my
creations, micro-processes my myriad indicative
signs,

---

[61] Sophocles (496-406 B.C.E.) : The ancient Greek tragedian
[62] Archelogos: In ancient Greek "Great Primordial Logos, or Word"

clarifies the patterns my mind is driving toward, by
which the
psyche and it hallucinations are discerned as
interfused
and separable, diverse and utterly united.

I do not hear him speak, yet feel the pressure of his
surpassing
intellect upon the circuitry of my neurons, and the
urging
of his palm and fingertips upon the hand by which
I write.

I do not know if these and other phenomena I
experience provide
evidence of supernatural communications between
dimensions
of an incommensurably expansive psyche, which
intertwine

at prescribed moments and locations. Perhaps
under certain
circumstances plaster crumbles, curtains lift, and
those of us
who most pertain through like-mindedness

congregate, at the same time one and several.
Subsequently,
further lines of mutuality become traversed, and it
might

be theorized that some singular organismic whole
could be assized

by which we would recognize at last that we are all
each other.
Such whelming joy, such articulation of longed-for
harmony,
would then, without surrender of the individual,
arise.

Whether that proximate Author of this present "I"
resides in
company of yet higher fellowship with entities of
greater
charge and mass, alone may claim "Primordial
Intellect" as his title,

or might constitute Self-finitizing of the very Deity,
however I
contrive to think of Him, or am contrived — as well,
these
manifold wonders which I find within — I

cannot doubt the truth which strikes me like a
mallet upon a
resounding bell, that Something's moving behind
the scenes
of which I am only dimly cognizant, some Other-
driven flight

to levels of reality obliquely perceived, reflections it
may be,
in which, if and when it might be granted me, I
shall abide,
then turn and find

these congeries of veterans, fellow-travelers on
Psyche's at
least functionally endless journey, at present
awaiting my
arrival—this, a question of consciousness
intensified

and focused on deeper, more enduring, and far
more sweeping
vistas, no longer opaque or screened, but radiant,
opalescent!
I shall emanate, or be emanated!

Yea, and I shall thrive!

4-6-09

Use Me Up

Use me up, O God, as if upon a sunlit summer day
I were joyously creating,

additioning to some praise of You, like singing
birds or dragonflies with glistening wings,

verdure misting or trees of massive foliage, like
hurrying bees and lilac blossoms thick-scented
upon a humid breeze,

like scurrying ants, and all thrumming, living
things.

Then take me quickly when I am spent, dispose of
who I was and what I did according to Your plan
for me,
and let me be exalted in my subsidence and my
sinking.

5-6-12

At the Speed of Light, I Swoon

O Great Goodness, deeper in than quark or muon,[63]
infinitely more distant than outermost moon,

faster than these staccato bursts of light, absolutely
motionless, more still than trees on stifling
August afternoons,

I sing unto Your magnificently extrapolated
Majesty! In such moods, I ask nothing. I don't even
wish to move.

I don't wish another heartbeat, nor not wish it. In
full-stop disanimation, or at the speed of light,
from bifurcated points of view,

I swoon.

9-12-14

---

[63] Quark, muon: Subatomic particles

Don't Let Me Become a Ghost

God, my God, don't let me become a ghost! Don't
relegate me to that host of the eternally dissatisfied,

nor division me, as the ancient Egyptians believed,
into a populous afterlife

of mummy, *ba*,[64] *ka*,[65] and *akh*,[66] nor arrange for me
to leave an ectoplasmic residue behind.

But unify my disparate selves, that a part, or parts,
of that community which now vie

for ascendency within my psyche, some of which
might wish to be the only "I,"

don't wander off into that darkness they even now
are prone to, and drop spread-eagled into vacuum

or bottomless abyss. Rather, empower me as a
complex yet whole personage to fly

---

[64] Ba: In ancient Egyptian "psychology," an aspect of the
person similar to the Western idea of soul
[65] Ka: In ancient Egyptian "psychology," an aspect of the
person similar to Western notions of an enlivening spiritual
essence capable of being imparted from one person to
another
[66] Akh: In ancient Egyptian "psychology," an aspect of the
person which has never incarnated in the explicated realm,
and which lives forever in a transfigured, or divine, state in
the highest spiritual world

far above those realms of nightmare and the
demonic, through clere-storied vistas of flaring
light,

and arrive within Your Land of Love, me, myself,
entire!

10-17-13

To Good Account

I am not able to heal the fissures and battered
aspects
of my make-up and life's experiences — certainly
not completely.

To achieve that intuited integration of a once-and-
future
Self, I need the Whole-making Power of Deity.

I will take that in as I am able, and trust that if I lift
up
all the scattered pieces of what I have achieved and
been,

God will mend me, turn everything I've undergone
to good account,

and receive me with joy, even with celebrity.

2-13-11

May God Be Gracious to You

(Adapted from the ancient Egyptian Coffin Texts)

May God be gracious to you at the staircase of your ascent to the sifting and the weighing.

May He be gracious to you at the Tribunal.

May He be gracious to you at the thresholds between the worlds, and at those serpent-sentried gates.

May He be gracious to you at the crossroads between two ways.

May He be gracious to you at all those places in which He may be gracious to you posterior to your funeral.

1-12-11

Surpassing Peace

(Adapted from an Eighteenth Dynasty Tomb
Inscription)

May you come and go as you please.
May you flit about on summer breezes.
May you rejoice in lakes and trees.
Your transitioning completed,
may you swoop and dart, just there brushing
water's gleam.
May you be encompassingly happy and find
surpassing peace.

5-11-12

Golden Palaces

O God, I want You to make me of gold, which
does not rust or tarnish:
fingers of gold, toes of gold, face of gold, golden
nose, golden hair and beard,
eyes of gold, throat of gold, neck, shoulders, torso,
arms, legs, hands and feet of gold,
back of gold, everything of gold, which does not
perish.
I want trees of gold, blades of grass of gold, golden
animals,
golden insects, golden birds, bushes of gold, golden
sky, golden earth,
golden water, sun, moon, stars of gold, loved ones,
even golden enemies,
buildings and furnishings of gold, oceans of gold,
golden sand,
food and drink of gold, golden all the senses.

And once everything is turned to gold — thoughts,
feelings, words, actions,
breathing, walking, sleeping, waking — and I am
reassured
that everything has been rendered into gold, and
will not blemish,
then I wish to see it all re-clothed in flesh, shell,
feathers, carapace,
yet re-created, all of it, lifted up, made to glow
of gold just beneath the surface,

and shout like horns of gold, golden trilling,
swarms and herds in golden
palaces re-envisioned for eternity, polished freshly,
buffed and inextinguishably
burnished.

1-29-12

Night Prayer

O God, at night when I drift down into those vast
concavities
where angels and demons brindle, clash, and
writhe,
then out upon the void, in that process becoming
vaporous,
and cease to be entirely,

guard that entity which You have breathed as me,
and with
Lightning and Your blinding Sword strike through
these
fantasies which fog and rise, grasp my hand, and
bring me
to Your Light!

8-14-10

A Prayer for Labor

Make that which I build today contribute, through
my
volition or by perforce, to this world of matter
and to some resonance of that, optimally
configured,
in realms of psyche and the spirit.

However incremental or diminutive, may what I
construct
issue forth in these: true and beautiful representations
of that which dwells in Mystery, or that eventuates
in
artifacts which,

depending upon the awareness of their users,
might become
translucent to Divinity. Let these shift this imaged
world a little in Your direction, that goodness,
light,
and joy, palpable and substantial,

might be recognized as reality corporeal. May
these, my

efforts on Your behalf, bring Your Kingdom nearer here, and There, reverberate in Your Eternity! This is

my deepest wish.

9-15-09

He Fits Us with Precision

That great merciful God knows our extremity of
darkness, and
drops beyond that into shadow so deep we cannot
track Him,

nor imagine where that goes, what inconceivable
profundity of
that-which-is He generates from there. We lose
Him in the
blackness.

Before the pressure of that abyssal crushes us, we
turn back. In
any case, He does not wish that fate for us, and
guides us to
His Brilliance,

which is higher up and brighter than anything we
can grasp. We
lose Him in that loftiness and dazzle too, but on a
better mission.

No matter. He makes Himself our size — well,
actually, much larger,

but still within our frames of reference. He meets us where we
need Him, and fits us with precision.

1-22-14

Totally Yield Up My Spirit

Here I am at that fabled last gasp,
at the end of everything.

Just one more breath, one sighed exhalation,
and I drop off into Infinity.

I don't want to go out there. Well, I do.
But in my present condition,

I'm not even remotely prepared. If I accomplish
this, I want some assurance I can keep

this particular rendition, or some, or any,
variation on the theme of being me.

Yet still, in God I could gape breathless.
I could fade to nothingness

as He does. Like Him, I might be multiplied
in disguise of loaves and fishes.[67]

---

[67] This is a reference to a miracle of Jesus' in which he multiplied loaves of bread and fishes for a large crowd of his listeners who had become hungry. The reference is from the New Testament Gospel of Luke, chapter 9, verses 12-17.

Or, like Him even more, I could become
His very Light-and-Darkness,

albeit no longer me as trace or vestige,
and totally yield up my spirit.

5-31-14

When to Ecstasy

When to ecstasy I have been hurled,
and known that one benevolent Immensity,
that stupendous Presence over-flowing I'm
impelled to denominate and indicate as
"God," I have been made as grave as iron,
entered into a state of wonderness, still
a man, yet so large and strangely deep
I cannot respirate or think. I cannot tell
you what I've heard or where I've been.
"Everything" and "Nowhere," is all that
I may venture.

10-14-05

Only Ever You

It was only ever You, and those close associates
You raised up by means of biochemistry "within"

and "outside" of me, for Whom I've loved and
lived—beyond this,

that wider world of driven things in thrall to
Empedocles'[68]
master-moves of Harmony and Strife.

It is only You to Whom I sing, Whom I adore most
fervently, to Whom I've dedicated my life,

all the epochs and episodes with which You've
graced me, whatever years, months, moments

more You have decreed for this, my earthly form.
I hope I have negotiated successfully enough

those pitfalls and illusions which You have cast
across my aspirations for advancement

by which You've tested my integrity and such
perspicacity of intelligence and talent

---

[68] Empedocles (c.490-c.430 B.C.E.): An ancient Greek pre-Socratic philosopher who taught that the Unity of Reality is achieved through a complementary movement and interfusing of two opposite cosmic principles—Harmony and Strife

as You have gifted me. I would say I've done about
the best I could within those contexts

wherein I initially arose and was subsequently
shaped,
and that all the aspects of my experience,

complex, riddled with paradox and ambiguity, as
well
as those that manifested more straightforwardly,

through which You made me real, and which You
caused
me to employ, produced, not perhaps perfection,

yet something You might recognize as contributing
to Your Joy, and as some further confirmation

of the Reason in the first place for Your becoming
Being!

6-1-14

The Error of Copernicus

The Hermeticists said, "The center of God is
everywhere;
His circumference is nowhere."

I say, His center might as well be here.

The Big Bang theory of the origin of the universe
proposes that the center for that event and
its aftermath is here and there.

I say, here and there is any where.

Where we are, You are, radiating Your Mystery
from our
interiors. The followers of Copernicus are in error.[69]

4-7-12

---

[69] Copernicus (1473-1543): The Polish mathematician and astronomer who proposed that the Earth revolves around the Sun, rather than vice versa. The psychological effect of his proposal was to "dethrone" the human being from the center of the universe, and, by implication, from the Deity's concern.

Intimate Divide

You are the sweep of light that gusts me upward
toward
the heights — not of course to this or any other sky.

In life we are in death. In death we are alive. And
even in
this darkness with which You've gifted me, I see
signs

of Your regard. I feel fully joy, and fly across that
infinite
expanse which constitutes our most intimate
divide.

3-17-07

Infinitely More than That

The toil of scholars in nooks and crannies of reality,
no matter how miniscule their compass,
is all worthwhile, and more than that.

The labor of patient artisans, no matter how remarked
or unrewarded, is all worthwhile, and more than
that.

All professions and careers, all works of any honest species,
pursued with excellence as their goal,
are all worthwhile, and more than that.

All of this will turn to frost or dust, or be
extinguished by a
bloated sun. No matter. What was done was done,
and was worthwhile, and considerably more than
that.

God will remember each productive act, and with what
intention it was performed. For Him it
was worthwhile, and infinitely more than that.

1-22-13

Debtors' Prisons

Jesus said there are debtors' prisons in Heaven,
cells in which
one sits alone owing others with no means to repay
them.[70]

But if a certain state of contrition is gained,
responsibility owned
up to, and the desire to make amends becomes
genuine,

I have heard that behind the scenes, unbeknownst
to debtors,
God is printing money in the basement.

7-21-14

---

[70] The reference is to the New Testament Gospel of Matthew, chapter 18, verses 23-35. My interpretation here represents a rather free adaptation and extension of the text.

The Eyes of God

The Eyes of God are liquid, glistening,
like those of does or seals.

The pupils are deep like bottomless wells,
and black as ravens' — inscrutable
and all-revealing,

or like the space between the stars, yet
not opaque, but sheening.

The Eyes of God are wet as seas. In them
are all thoughts and feelings.

Above all else, the Eyes of God are kind,
and very, very peaceful.

12-8-14

What Is That Splendor?

Oh! What is that Splendor which overfloods the
world
and makes all things joyful even in their weeping?

Oh! It is a Light that momentary suffering cannot
obscure,
which resolves in ecstatic trans-harmonics, sudden
leapings,

all that everything has undergone — these shadows
and
these gleamings — justified in this very instant,
triumphed, and completed!

3-9-16

Lyre

I am neither good nor wise as some, Thy creatures
most esteemed,
nor always kind, nor have I realized those most
exalted mystic dreams,
neither sublimest incantations of the intellect,
which nonetheless I
touch upon occasion,
nor the genius of Thy artists gained, nor political
power, nor wealth
obtained.
Yet when Thou playest me, full-chorded or single-
strained,
and sighest through such qualities as these by
which Thou framest me,
Thy Breath whelms within my chest, and I sing,
trembling, as I am able.
This is my passion because it is Thou that assayest
and I Thou playest.
I know this embodied tryst is flawed and passing—
some portion
nevertheless of Thy Magnificence and Thy
Radiance.

1-19-05

Ghosts and Shadows

Dazed

We occupy this eerie landscape over which the cast-back
light of a world actualizing our vanishment plays

as if across an inert mirror or a death-still lake. We have
no way to gauge that mind-evaporating

illumination toward which we slide unrecoverably,
somnambulant, torporous, dazed.

5-21-15

Equally as Real

There was not a puff of wind or breath of breeze
when the sickle moon slid sharp and gleaming
through the darkening trees,

and took its station on a cloudless eve, paused as
if observing me, held my gaze, then turned
its crescent round

and sprinted up to apogee. Of course, I realize
that all of that was me, whoever that is really,
making magic, bounding

through the cluttered things, arranging these for
my own safety and convenience. But still, who
was that watching me

as if it were the moon? Not the me that witnessed
it. Undoubtedly some other self sundered from my
identity, yet equally as real.

7-21-15

Minerva

Minerva[71] flies at dusk on dove-grey wings. She alights
from some Otherwise
upon the stony throne of mind, by Medusa's daylight
shrieking fossilized,
just before mentation re-liquefies and slides beneath
penumbraed seepage of the night.
She inserts herself into this: dissolution of ego-consciousness,
and, within a livid vision dives,
commands with that the animal soul to sink into abeyance,
awakens spirit with Her chirping and Her cinder eyes.
Alert and vivid now, animated by Her unearthly Psyche,
the holy soul emerges from inside,
rises up with Her, surveys its mortal life, knifes forward

---

[71] Minerva: The ancient Roman goddess more or less equivalent to the Greek Athena—among other things, goddess of Wisdom

through its pains and pleasures,
discovers an unnerving Joy, and in the darkness
thrives!

11-7-15

Most Intimate

Do you hear it lisping on the underside,
close to your ear?
Skin prickling, getting your senses up,
putting you on alert—not fear
exactly, although that's a part of it. More
like something wonderful drawing near—
dreadful, life-ending, renovating entirely,
something heart-rendingly joyful...
and very weird.
And you feel a certain trembling eagerness
for it, like a yearning for bells pealing,
or chanting somewhere in the distance, muffled
by the trees, but present immediately, just here—
like nothing you've heard or known before,
except maybe a loved one's voice in the
morning, or the breath of
a child on your cheek.
It's sublime and sleek. It's not a serpent's hiss
or a rushing of wind. It's enunciated, but
nothing in a language you
could ever sing or speak.

Then it's inside you. Probably always was.
But now you're listening.

You are electrified.

Didn't you think God would eventually find you,
and wish with you to be most intimate?

12-15-14

Sometimes There Is Knocking

Sometimes there is knocking from the inside of a
bolted door,
or a murmuring which issues from between the
door-foot
and its limen,

at times, a scattering of dust across the floor of who
I say I am,
or refracted light fanned out beneath the board
above the
sill. I am

frozen in my tracks, goose-fleshed, re-apprised that
some
Otherworld dwells within the many-divisioned
House of
Psyche, by acts of will

contained from spilling out into the corridors I
have built and
pace, afraid to let that out, or in, terrified it will
erupt, engulf,
and still me.

I am afraid to unlatch those numinous doors I
know conceal
bottomless pits, careening lights, paralyzed by the
thought
of the who's those might comprise

that I have locked away to save my sanity, my
more or less
familiar earth-side self. What right have these
intruders
to my life?

Should I summon all my courage, risk psychosis by
inviting
Wholeness of inassimilable proportions?[72] Perhaps
that
doesn't matter.

Someday I will have to.

6-16-14

---

[72] This is a reference to the depth psychological, or Jungian, notion that the human psyche is called upon to integrate all opposites, including the "light" and "darkness" within it, into an ego-transcending whole, which Jung termed the Self.

Ghost

I am not only who I seem.
I am haunted — deeply, truly, irredeemably.
I am a labyrinth of indeterminable dimensions.
I cannot tell how far down I go beneath this
heaved-up
surface, where I breathe and speak.
There is more to me than can be shown here, or
seen.
I am a ghost, on an errand obscure to me.
When I leave, I will enter...Reality...or so I believe.

7-24-15

Hylas

Hylas,[73] strayed from Herakles' side, got lost in a
pathless wood,
thickly brambled, ladled deep in shadows.

He came upon a glade, within it an algaed pool
half-clogged
with reeds and verdant lily pads.

He knelt at water's edge, dipped cupped hand to
drink the plashy
fluid. Suddenly that murky green

broke in silver rings across the surface of the water.
Seven ivory
nymphs rose to their waists, streaming

black and tawny hair, so long it fanned and floated
on that swaying.
Hylas started, ceased his leaning.

He almost stood. But three placed clammy hands
upon his skin,
softly digited, yet more than playfully insistent.

---

[73] Hylas: In ancient Greek legend, Hylas was the lover of the
demigod Herakles, the great laborer and civilization-builder.
Hylas was lost on an island and presumed dead during the
voyage of the Argonauts in quest of the golden fleece.

All cooed and soothed, promising an underwater
rule of ample
rushes, and docile, gliding fish.

They cocked their heads and, slanting, smiled.
They grasped their
breasts and gently urged them toward his opening
lips.

He swooned and pitched into the pond. Once in,
they drove him
deeper down, until his sip

upon the brink became his deep submergence and
his drowning.
We say, Poor Hylas, tricked by love

into his death. But I say, his death eventuated in his
crowning in that
magic land below-above

the surface of this world, where everyone is
recompensed with
immortality, and all the lost are found.

4-13-14

Bathroom Mirror

Stand some space of time before your bathroom
mirror,
lower than the ceiling, right above the basin.

Look into your eyes without remorse or fear, not
considering
the truth of what you think you think.

Hold the gaze of that which reflects you back to
you, that similitude
from mercury and shimmering glass, unblinking.

Soon or late, this visaged trick of light will clear all
obscurations,
deliver you to terror and elation —

vistas open of the you's you've been, or are right
now in
innumerably altered states, estranged
congregations

of angels, bacteria, rocks, minerals, apes, unsettling
images conveying
un-prefigured revelations

of ancestral lineages traced deeply all the way to
Nature's irreducible
matter-of-factness. There it is, right there, staring
through-

and-past you as if you'd never been. You'll feel a chill now, like
Dickenson's "zero to the bone,"[74] who intimately knew

that schizoid serpent in the grass which neared, footed, and slid
past her. There's nothing more for you to do.

Just watch the eyes behind your eyes reveal a certain pealing back,
layer-by-layer, a falling off in infinite

regress, forever, the direction of total nulling. Nothing, then, of you
is left. Where are you, creature of the mirror,

and what is your condition? What it has always been: superficiality,
now awed and disappeared within the vastness of Divinity.

7-3-06

Impassable, Muted Mysteries

Those I loved, and those I knew, who gave me joy,
as I did these,

are whisked away, disapparate, like lifting haze
above the fields,
and now are almost without presence,

except when memory rushes up, and presses on
my consciousness,
like lucent breeze upon the cheek,

or like soul-refreshing dawns in June, and I can
hear them speak to me
as they were used to do, see their gestures,

feel their laughter against my skin, know them
again
as they were then, and be that me

I was — am, and am no longer, now that they and I
are gone —
the way they dressed,

the chairs in which they sat, the things they
handled I
handle still, the air they breathed,

which we once shared, in which we quarreled,
sighed,
and played, the earnestness

of our conversations. Well, they are where all
things go,
creatures of a moment, briefly graced with
being here,

then raised and hushed above into that limitless
and
unechoing Stillness

in which we all will end, as we began — impassable,
muted Mysteries.

12-25-14

And I Could Fall in-Love with Death

In your jet-black depths of smoothed-back feathers
I could be
lost, as in those sable pools of Houris' eyes,[75]
cool as glass and glistening, yet staring without
sight
like fishes, fathomless, abyssal.

I could fall with loping wolf-like strides of ancient
Celts
into their tinseled Otherworld, breathless,
creeping down the streets of Rome, unsure if they
had died
and entered realms of Fairy.[76]

These encountered serried ranks of togate senators
in snow-
white winding sheets, seated like a frozen wall of
ocean spume on frigid marble thrones, still as
fields of sculpted cattle,

or like those fabulous, transfigured dead at the
other ends

---

[75] Houris: In the Qur'an, the eternal virgins reserved for Muslim men in Paradise
[76] Realms of Fairy: This is a reference to the Celtic sack of Rome in 390 B.C.E., and the idea that any number of their raids into Mediterranean territory and even into Anatolia represented their attempts to find the entrance to the Otherworld.

of lead pipe offering tubes thrust beneath the earth,
down which wine was poured in ghost-appeasing
rituals of libation.

And I could fall in-love with death.

Or I might pod as steaming meat with
reverberating whales,
blood sliding slag-like beneath encrusted
hides, miles and miles below, soundless, dropping
into
Arctic night, where cerebration ceases.

Or, like long-tressed Druids,[77] I could spread my
arms, bare
white breastbone, phasing into spirit,
shape-shift into raven guise, sprout midnight
pinions, push off
and glide on musty exhalations

of the clamming corpse, inch upward, clod-by-clod,
from ice-
bound barrow, and shed this detritus of the body,
glide up toward that corroded mirror moon,
death-enchanted,
crosiered, bronze-encapsulate,

clattering, bone-to-socket, slide through swollen
shadows with

---

[77] Druids: The Celtic priesthood

Sylvanus[78] and his fleshless hound, or with mystics
of all tribes and races strive with main and might
to thin and thin to
nothingness, subside into the One,

and make an end, no longer "I," some other thing,
uncanny,
perhaps infinite, and without misgivings,

fall in-love with death.

3-8-09

---

[78] Sylvanus (or Silvanus): The ancient Roman god of
boundaries, particularly those between the wild forests and
the cultivated land

Soft as Sifted Ash

Someone's here with me. I can feel it,
someone leaking light, pressed out smooth,
flitting thinly, with ankle bells tinkling
like ice cubes in a tumbler, calling me,
wraith-like, from within. I can almost see her
by means of inconclusive extrusions — room
after room, corridors, atriums, through
bricks, ashlar blocks, cement and plaster,
almost in silence, not a living voice nor an
actually audible stirring — except for these
tintinabulate, fabulous heart-vanquishing bells.
Now I feel edgeless, soft as sifted ash.

4-17-05

Iulia

What was Iulia thinking, age forty-three, wrinkles
beginning to split the corners of her eyes —
these, from years of laughter and gracious smiles —
so many parties in her garden on spring and
summer nights
at her villa on the northern shore of Lake Moeris?[79]

Because of her illness, coming on for three years,
her eyes had gotten brighter, or at least more
prominent, moister, and more compassionate than
before. Still the aristocrat, though. She held her chin
high.

She still wore grape-cluster earrings. Her maid
continued to dye her hair black even as her skin
gradually paled to a chalk-like white,

and pinned it up with gold in the latest fashion. She
was lonelier now, due to her illness, and her
husband was away more often on imperial
business.
Did she think, perhaps without self-pity,
"I am now a case of faded glory"?

What was she thinking as she sat for her mummy
portrait in that same garden that had once been her
stage, where with a blending of a sense of

---

[79] Lake Moeris: In ancient times, a large freshwater lake in the
Egyptian Faiyum Oasis southwest of the Nile Delta.

superiority and authentic kindness she had
entertained
so many of her neighbors, foreign dignitaries,
senators' wives from Rome?

She sat there in the sun, holding a pose, her long
neck slightly forward and to the side, her italic nose
and high cheekbones angled three-quarters toward
the painter,
managed and held a shadow of her former smile,

restrained by pain but nonetheless still warm, more
sincere perhaps than any smile she'd ever smiled
before.

She knew what mummies looked like—hideous
emaciated mockeries of the lives which had
animated once thinking, feeling bodies—people
once, who'd played
and joked and been angry, hurt, jealous, forgiving,
people who'd
had a sense of purpose, people who had loved.

Her portrait on a painted acacia plank would be
inserted into those awful wrappings that would
conceal the leathered corpse, and mask the
withered visage they would make of her face in the
so-called "House of Beauty."

The painting would be a mixture of her as she had
been and as she'd become—a kind of maturing and

fruition. It would represent her essence in that
world to which she was succumbing,

a better world than this, no doubt, with more
luxuriant viburnum and more costly fountains,
with even grander and more enjoyable parties. In
time, whatever that might mean over there,
her husband
would join her. She'd had no children. Maybe
there would be orphans to adopt.

At any rate, this mask would be the face by which
she would be signified "Iulia" to her new
companions, and by which she would be presented
to the gods.

Iulia was going on a fabulous and mysterious
journey, yet one she also dreaded. She'd always
loved the fabulous and mysterious. Since she'd
been a child, she'd treasured Ovid's
"Metamorphoses" and Homer's "Odyssey."

Now she was going to step inside and live within
the myths. Yet she would pass into the fabulous
with more than fear: regret — leaving the birds, the
Lake, that fantastic Egyptian sun — most of all her
garden and her husband.

Feeling tired too early in the day — it was barely
afternoon — she dismissed the painter, set their next

appointment, let a servant show him to the garden door.

Three months later Iulia slipped from life quietly in her bed by the window shortly before dawn.

After sixty days at the House of Beauty, what was left of her earthly substance was interred in a low-cut limestone tomb.

Two thousand years passed. Her mummy was discovered and thrown out with the trash. The mask was recognized as striking, however, and sold to a museum.[80]

I wonder if Iulia is still thinking, and, if she is, of what. I wonder if she's happy, as she certainly deserved to be. My guess is either that, or she's moved on beyond the possibility of my imagining her
as Iulia in any form.

11-21-13

---

[80] During the Roman Period of ancient Egypt, many Roman residents of Egypt accepted the native practice of mummification as a preparation for their souls' eternal lives beyond the grave.

An Exorcism

She was there, right beside my chair in that
upstairs
sitting room — Gary's mother —

after he'd left for the kitchen to get us some iced
tea,
after he'd calmed down sufficiently, after

that whoosh! and his gasp, "She's here!" She was
right beside me,
under the lamp, creaking the floor boards
rhythmically:

eek-eek, eek-eek. I've lived with floor boards most
of my life.
They only do that if

someone's shifting their weight back and forth
intentionally.
I talked to her as if she'd been a counselee.

I told her I had no idea what she was going
through,
of course, but that she'd died in that car crash
instantly,

and she couldn't come back, that Gary would be
fine,
that I was certain they would see each other again,

and that, if she could see a light, I thought she
should move
toward it. The floor went

silent. Gary returned with our drinks. He said,
"She's gone!"
with relief. I said, "I believe she's moved to
a higher level."

She was never felt in that house again. The
hauntings ceased.
I felt sad, but I think I did the right thing.
I hope her joy increased.

11-4-14

Un-grieved

He lay spraddled over the sweated sheets. In the massiveness
of his death throes he'd occupied the entire length and breadth
of the bed.

Moments ago he'd been a living man, gigantic in centrality for
his family, now somehow even vaster in that location with
his exit.

This was stated clearly by the ring of chairs around the bed —
as well, their occupants' varied expressions of helplessness
and despair.

Two were silent. Three were sobbing. One was frantic. I was asked
to bless the dead. I opened the pages of *The Common Book of Prayer*

and read. I closed with some of my own words of hope and
consolation, and all adjourned to the living room

with attached kitchen for coffee and cake, temporarily abandoning

that catastrophe in back to its freight of the
miraculous and
the doomed.

They seated me on the sofa, the wife-and-mother
who'd been
making coffee when I'd come in, the son who'd, at
the same
instant, been gazing

out the window, and the six who'd been seated
round the cooling
cadaver of that titan in the sweat-soaked bed.
They'd called
me, and I'd come, too late

to help him contemporaneously through that fatal
gate, though I
believed he'd still been within earshot, standing in
some shadow
on the Other Side

as I'd intoned the liturgy and benediction. I turned
to comforting
the survivors who'd watched him expire as the
darkness
opened wide

and swallowed him. The wife was shaken but
performed her hostess
duties well. The son attempted humor. The

daughters were in
earnest.

The frantic one collapsed beside me and squeaked.
She said they'd
had a fight, her father and she, three days earlier,
that she'd told
him she never

wanted to see him again. Like me, she'd arrived too
late for the great
man's quittance, and was bitterly lamenting the
fulfillment of her
wish. She was consumed

with the irony of this, and by paroxysms of regret. I
told her he was
still in the vicinity, that he could simulate her
sorrow — more, that
he had assumed

a position more intimate to her than her own
anguish, that there were
no secrets between the living and the dead, and
that sooner than
she might think

they would be in each other's arms again. She
smiled through her tears
and began to calm. Then she and two of her sisters

confided in me a long-guarded talent inherited in
the female line of
their family — psychic abilities — among these,
clairvoyance,
precognition, and communing with ghosts.

That's a story I won't pursue here. What remains is
to express my
on-going astonishment years later at that
remarkable afternoon and
the post

I was called to by strangers. All that I'd said and
done in that little
house in the country I'd thoroughly believed.

I left it not merely believing, but incomparably un-
grieved.

2-16-14

We Should Not Roam

When we have died, we should not roam those
shadowed corridors
which tightly bind and trace the contours of that
world from
which we've been expelled,

those disconcerting door-less halls with echoing
stairwells leading up
and down, round and round, behind the walls, that
never yield
to greater light, that smell

of spices and formaldehyde, narrow or wide,
carpeted, tiled, or
strewn with rubble, with miles and miles of ceiling
pipe above,
but no Exit sign to tell

where we might leave the maze. There's no way
out except by mind.
No, not mind — the heart, or insight, which alone,
by imaging
some other else,

can cure us of our yearning to find re-entrances
through cinder-block,
stone, or linen scrim into that bright and urgent
realm whose
bustlings now are muffled

by this unassailable boundary on the inner side. We
must close our
eyes and stop our ears to those and what we loved
and hated,
and delve —

deep, deeper, deepest — to that airless place which
first gave birth
to us, beyond all finitude and barriers, and find
that glaring
Fundament

of Light which dissolves these, or lifts us up away
from all such
throttled species, and repositions us within a vast
Benevolence.

1-14-13

The Darkly Dead

Sometimes in the autumn I think of the darkly
dead,
who, beneath the earth, abide in some ungodly
fashion,

haunt desolate places like the basements of old
houses,
decaying woods and rural railroad tracks — and

send up unwholesome vapors that blacken trees,
blight
gardens, reek of rancid sweat and cabbages.

I don't know how they wound up in such a
situation,
but I pray Almighty God for my and their
salvation.

5-6-14

Disincarnate Psyches

When disincarnate psyches, fragments or
projections of these
body forth into our dimension of time, space, and
matter

from behind the filmy sheet of Lethe which marks
the limits of our
realities, they may press so forcefully against that
screen that

it bulges startlingly toward us, takes the shape of
he or she who
wishes to be noticed, and, depending on the
strength of their capacities

and desires, may create a two- or three-
dimensional manikin —
in the first case, like a moving photograph, in the
second, like a
hologram.

Or the soul may intrude this-world-ward with so
much longing that
the film detaches from its background, slaps up
close around the
psychic fragment,

and depicts with such similitude that person, that
we may hear them

walking, even speaking. The temperature around
them drops
dramatically,

and, more often than not, they're lit up by some
source which they
themselves are generating, or which accompanies
that gleaming
by which they've been cascaded

into our inner sight, or even as if they'd become
material objects.
Perhaps they're not entirely here when they project
themselves,
but only images.

I'd like to think that's the case, and that they're
safely in some higher
clime of consciousness and being than they seem to
us, and, as a
consequence, significantly gladder.

2-28-15

Oddments of the Psychic Realm

You know, I don't agree with F.W.H. Myers'[81]
claim that his work
with oddments of the psychic realm relegates
religious hopes
to sugar-coated wishes.

I do not doubt the truth of the majority of his
findings. But I still
conclude that the dead who want to stay
communing with their
loved ones in this in-between of his

need to find a more exalted life than automatic
writing, raps on
tables, hauntings, and the like. They need to seek a
greater elevation,
and take the high road to Divinity.

2-25-15

---

[81] F.W.H. Myers (1843-1901): A pioneer in a more expansive
view of the human psyche than is contemplated by most
contemporary schools of psychology. Myers took what has
become known as the field of parapsychology with the
utmost seriousness.

The Merely Archaeological

That which was once alive and vital, with time
stiffens
and decays into the merely archaeological.

The Spirit moves on from form to form, and
presently
even we might be *au current* and eminently
fashionable.

But beware! What we consign to dust and rubble
has
never truly died. It may rear up in the blink
of an eye,

and render us forgettable.

11-2-14

Slip Sideways into Midnight

Night pours into the pastel hollow of fading day
like thick
wine into an empty drinking cup — say, a *kylix*.[82]
The bowl is shallow, thin-walled, delicate almost as
a breeze,
with two floating out-flung hand-grips.
The interior of the cup is glazed a featureless black
except
for that spectral disk of orange centered at its nadir

like an image of the sun abandoned in deep space.
As night
flows in, it floods and drowns that wavering
luminescence,
the daylight realm and all that stands for, but does
not
completely occult it. On the cup's outside,
two eyes gaze at the companions of the imbiber —
when it's
turned and tipped, those reclining opposite — not
precisely hostile,

nor entirely uncaring — more like Nature — through
it, its

---

[82] Kylix: A thin-stemmed, wide-brimmed, and shallow ancient
Greek drinking cup often used in the late night parties known
as symposia, during which, among other things, issues in
politics, religion, and philosophy were often discussed

Creator, observing your progressive intoxication
and
that of your companions.
Accept the vision that meets you Eye-to-eye. Drink
the night
that makes the light slide eerily and shimmer.
Day is done. Your cares are finished. It's time for
you to liquefy,
then slip sideways into midnight.

6-18-14

The Siren's Song

The Sirens' song[83] comes from beyond this world or
any other,
and so is hated by those with work to do, all of us
with agendas.

We imagine them as monsters in order to keep
ourselves intact,
thereby, pass on sublimity and splendor. It doesn't
matter.

We shall all hear their song at last, and slip beneath
the waves
in wonder.

4-22-14

---

[83] The Sirens' song: In ancient Greek mythology, the Sirens
(part women and part birds), through their mesmerizing
singing, lured human beings (archetypally, sailors) to their
deaths, and consequently to transfigured states of
consciousness and being on the "other side" of reality as we
know it.

The Soul Sinks Down into the Earth

The soul sinks down into the earth
and is lost from view.

Some souls become trapped in underground
caves and caverns.

These must be found and rescued.

Some souls sink down into the earth
and pass right through.

11-20-13

Thy Deity's Subtle Glimmer

When I, secluded from thy sight, have sought thee
recent risen
from the night, bedclothes cast upon thy marbled
floor
dismissively, or footboard trailing,

exhaling redolence of starch, perfume, thy sweated
vents, naked
thou, inviolate before this morning's flood of peach
and
white, curtains lightly sailing,

I have observed thee pass from bed to dresser,
coffee take, thy day
unfurling, thy upper arms goose-fleshing,
unremorseful
for thy providence or fate,

thou ensconced before thy capacious mirror,
crystalline yet oddly
like a prism, refracting incandescent grape and
mango hues,
ice and fire simultaneously,

and, while reflecting thee, thy body and thy
countenance, something
more, some aetheric psychic substance, true to thee,
and yet
evocative of what I take to be

thy deity's subtle glimmer, indeterminate flash or
mercurial shiver
round-against the supple, fawn-like skin, coronaed
at thy head,
and thy auroral shimmering.

I have felt upon occasions such as these, watching
thee, rapt—indeed,
amazed, ecstatic—some unplumbed disparity
between thy
shuddered chill and thy exaltation

across the breast of ancient day, thy minutest
voyaging traversing
tracts of waste vaster than Antarctic or interstellar
space
within thy unreflexioned sitting, intricate

subatomic hazes, thy soul with spirits face-to-face
within the glinting
glaze, so many thee's of thee's self-displaying,
tracked back
or inward toward anterior portrayals when thou
wast other
than thou art at present, existentiated nonetheless,
thy diety localized,
insistent on thy multitudes of meanings,
thy depths and superficialities—

both of these revealing some termless profundity
thou art regardless of thy

contemporary preening — some infinite regress, hammering
beak to pellet, against the magic

of the glass, thy mind, or Mind, inscripting thus:
"Thee as me, as thee —
as well, these illimitable interlopers intervening, assigned identities,
fiery mists and migrant vagueries."

This transpires while thou attendest to thy ministrations and these
instants re-presenting now's which never have existed,
were not begotten ever, and were instantly erased.

Then storms of sudden light I witness, trivial at inception, nickering about
thy ears and eyes — moments after, igniting gilded nimbus
circumferencing thy crown, a blaze of writhing snakes with gnashing
mandibles enflamed, consuming, as I gaze, thy countenance
well-renowned, thy raven locks combusting, thy midnight
tresses borne aloft as ash, whiffling up, defying gravity,

and thou art utterly transformed. Enchanted thou, as thy incendiary

deity, flaring outward, thy corporeality vanished in
torrents
of lava from within, immolation of thy teeth,

ascendeth. It is now thou shoutest, bounding
trumpets, or art shouted —
and thy body banished.

Sighing, as if momentarily distracted, returnest to
thy toiletries,
brush-fisted, oblivious to thy passing, which I,
occulted from thy
vision, have most assuredly witnessed
and enacted.

8-29-04

Bell-Krater[84] Depicting the Fate of Europa and Sarpedon: Red-figure, c. 400-380 B.C.E.

In a rococo lawn chair, stuffed with Persian
pillows,
out in that night that never sees dawn,
clothed in Iranian pajamas, cap Anatolian, the
Queen
of the West, Europa, reclines, waiting to be drawn
into atrocity
by some psychic announcement of unrectifiable
events in the East. It's coming alright. Indeed, it's
just arrived!
She's startled, in shock, then shattered.

Her man- and maid-servants, four of these,
respond
to the vision she's witnessing with a predictable
range of human dispositions:

the hand-maiden to her right, propped by the chair,
slides
her eyes left, unable or unwilling to pose more
dramatically;

---

[84]Krater: A large ancient Greek storage vessel for liquids,
usually unmixed wine. In this case, it is what is termed a bell-
krater because of its bell-like shape.

the male in the center stands gaping, fingers spread
wide;
the one on the right has dropped to his knees,
clasping his hands

in a gesture of prayer; the maid further right, just
under
the vision, bearing a platter, freezes, retracts her
neck like a turtle, then rolls her eyes up toward that
lowering blackness.

One believes that as the vision descends in that
stark
darkness, where Heaven and Earth become
indistinguishable, all, stupefied initially, will
suddenly
spring into a flurry of distraught behaviors: "Is
there nothing
to be done?" —
then, helplessness, the recognition that there isn't.

Through that hypnotic jet, fore and aft, winged
Sleep and
Death[85] are approaching from somewhere
beyond the full moon, transporting the nude corpse
of her
life-shorn son, Sarpedon.[86]

---

[85] Sleep and Death: In ancient Greek mythology, Sleep and
Death were brothers.
[86] Sarpedon: An ancient Greek hero of the Trojan War

They're soaring down from that lofty gloom, where nothing
is except human consciousness into the midst of
Europa's midnight excursion on the lawn.

Wordless, their duty done, Sleep and Death will lift silently
back into the timelessness and infinity from
which they've issued, leaving Europa like a fly in
amber, alone —
her mind, her emotions — the only act, or series thereof,
that's ever mattered, or ever will exist.

7-1-14

Something!

All these creatures and scenes that shift surface-
ward in dreams at midnight, wide-eyed visions at
noon, condensations breathed in on summer
evenings,

these intuitions, violent insights, answers to riddles
posed by inner sphinxes, guardian gods or angels,
monsters, perhaps, or demons —

Where do you think they come from?
What do they suggest to you?
And what do you suppose dwells in that obvious
abysm beneath your feet?

Something!

2-25-15

Her Mystery

Irrepressible even yet, she is limitlessly shape-
shifting,
form-to-form, ensorcelled — in this exulting,
at least initially — though she might be observed to
become
increasingly dispirited, echoing concavities, and
haunted,
still composing exoteric things within her waking
dream — to some extent aware of this — being
shadowed,
shadowing herself from room to room with a
certain
hurried padding of unshod feet, ankles, glinting
bells, hems flashing, heels absconded at these
ghostly
lintels, glimmerings through the plastered walls,
darkness
falling within those bottomless canyons of her
bewilderment and mystery.

2-25-05

A Haunting

Shouting unproudly, this livid spirit cracked,
evacuated the
mildewed host like an aromatic fish gone green
about the gills,

and commenced a hollow haunting in which
nightmares pooled,
and inexplicit terrors drew. That which spoke of
"I" slid

Hell-ward, trussed. It wetted the twisted sheets at
parting, weeping
blood and myrrh.

With little ease or respite, that once most cherished
intimacy was
breached. The soul slipped out and up beneath the
eaves.

Naked now, it hugs these ice-encrusted gutters,
shivering fins and
teeth, waiting anxiously for the morning, a sighting
of those beloveds still

warm in meat and skin, and of life without the
body whimpers thinly.

3-26-04

Persephone[87]

I.

She was assaulted by this blooming blackness, shot
up,
out-blown, this unlit mist, some coagulated
unbelonging
to the day at noon,

a welling, raven lump, rucked-up, alien, displacing
sky
and sun, which rent the hill-top sod, self-animate,
uninterested
in the lilting view, obtruding,

a certain instant freezing, wringing heat from
throttled air,
condensing this into iridium in plutonic
oscillations, a purple
smoking, obfuscating

---

[87] Persephone: The ancient Greek goddess of the Underworld, who was abducted by Hades and forced into marriage with him. Persephone—also called "The Maiden," or the "Kore," in order to avoid pronouncing her name—was a goddess of life, who was permitted by Zeus to return to the earth plane for nine months out of the year in order to cause all living things to flourish. She returned to the Underworld during the winter months. This is the seasonal version of the Persephone myth. On a deeper or more spiritual interpretation, she was the Great Goddess Herself, Mistress simultaneously of death and life.

that idyllic scene, deathly framing of the same, brittling the
grass, those wind-configured oaks, pines,
cypresses — these,
green as locusts or spring-fresh shoots,

a black flaming stark against that brightened high empyrean,
where lazy waves of blue entwined with mirrored photons,
anterior to that doomsday dancing out to vacuum,

that humid meadow half-liquefied by light and diaphanous,
a cacophony of wild flowers, rife with butter yellows,
water-color hues, the whole rambunctious rambling
drowsily exuding.

She was playing there before that came at her, homing, acquiring
directionality,
made straight for her, shredding, tearing, drove across the lawn,
stunned and seized her, quivering.

She was a girl; unknown to her the back of a man's hand, rough-knuckled,
sprigs of hair exfoliate on the upper digits. He brushed

the soft-as-iris epithelium of her inner thigh,
goose-fleshed
at his savage baring of her ample breasts,

her nipples stiff as sticks, then hauled her inward,
hand-over-fist
to his searing source, at one and the same time
obliteration
and bliss.
Dark unglinting enveloped her, and his rock-
hardness, vice-like
grip around her throat and wrists, prohibiting all
resistance.
She saw the world of light flash by, then Earth's
underside closed
above her. Lost in death, she would never make a
full recovery.

We are chastened, all of us abducted, ravaged at
our very cores,
subjugated utterly, driven into midnight wastes,
and smothered.
Like Persephone, however, we live on and further,
adapt to changed
conditions, more knowing and more sober.

II.

Anxious beyond measure, and enraged, the mother
sought her
daughter across the stony rind of Earth,[88]
dual torches darting, flaring, weaving, clenched
tight in gnarled
fists, dripping fiery gobbets as she swooped,
pelted, charged.
In the end, she learned the truth: Death may not be
averted, even
by the innocence of youth.
Still, she appealed to Him Who permits, or even
machinates,
whatsoever is thought, felt, known—
being and its negation. She appealed to Father
Zeus.

III.

Rigid, rimed with ice, Persephone sat beside her
frigid captor upon
a chthonic throne, entranced, catatonic, his massive
gravitational hand
like glaciers and crevasses, penetrating to the bone,
her flesh
refrigerated, bruised black-and-blue by his
manhandling—

---

[88] The mother is Demeter, goddess of agricultural abundance,
especially grain.

316

as well, by frost and still-life snow.
The scene
before her may scarcely be recited — a cave-like
pitch, which
fell away to indeterminate depths — passing,
barely by her noticed,
captives with exaggerated eyes, like those of
starving cats, glazed as
if filmed with glistening plates of crystal or of
brass,
some startled, locked in-place like that, like the
eyes of statues gazing
off, unseeing, upon what they'd witnessed last —
some terrible death,
some landscape of unspeakable depravity, an
overwhelming
thought or feeling, some unfinished task,
regret, or failure of achievement —
these along with "gliders" flitting round the roof
like rabid bats.

Orpheus came and left, empty-handed of his
Eurydice.[89]
Odysseus slew a sheep, drained its blood, spoke
briefly

---

[89] Orpheus and Eurydice: In ancient Greek mythology,
Orpheus, the oracular founder of a Mystery Religion, traveled
to the Underworld in order to try to resurrect Eurydice, the
woman he loved. He failed in this attempt.

with his mother, Agamemnon,[90] Achilles —
distraught,
turned back, headed for Penelope.

IV.

Zeus acknowledged the mother's grief and outrage,
contrived to shift his forearm,
sent word to have Persephone released for nine
months at a term.
When Demeter reached toward her child, ascended
freshly from the deep,
intending to clutch her, weeping, to those breasts
by which, in infancy,
she had nourished her so eagerly, Persephone hung
back, no tear escaping
ungladdened eye, trickling salty effluence to
trembling lip.
She was not angry; she was changed. Everything
was different now —
the sun in permanent eclipse for her, jet-bodied,
corona streaming
radioactive, issuing cerberic vapor, trees charred
corpses
at the stake, grass cinder-grey,
flowers stripped clean of life, minus all their former
pageantry,
her mother wild and strange. It took sometime

---

[90] Agamemnon: The chieftain who led the Greeks in the
Trojan War

before she could see in color.
Finally, she was able.
Yet her joy did not return. Ever after a kohlish tint clung,
stubborn as unending night, around her eyes, her pupils growing
ever larger until they overwhelmed the whites.
When November came,
she subsided, reappeared
each spring.

V.

No one dared to ask her how her marriage was, or how she found the life below.
She herself presented evidence enough. When she walked among those
divinities, they did not look her in the eyes, did not speak her name. Evasively,
they called her "Kore."

Across millennia, it was noticed that she warmed a bit by August.
Then, one year, a summer evening, when the air was damp and close,
her granite sheathing cracked, slipped down, then exploded from her skin
in a shower of shards and splinters. Then stepped forth a semblance of
the girl that she had been, bewildered, beheld her

mother consumed by
grief,
lingering long ages since,
ran to her, fell upon her mother's knees, laid her
head
there, wept inconsolably.
Without recourse she was forced to return to her
kingdom
of the ghostly dead.
However, now that she had come awake, she
realized
the full extent of disruption
between her living meat and her post-mortem fate.
That intervening void was
infinite,
unbridgeable, no intermediary steps or fractions by
which she could
calculate, or orient the self while conveying this
from one setting to
its opposite via radical administration.
Rather,
dramatic discontinuity reigned — the child alive,
pleromatic with significance,
empowered by this, laboring toward completion —
full stop:
automaton, disincarnation, a stripping of all that
constitutes the human,
reduced to breathless stone, personhood
extinguished.

VI.

Even so, something had occurred — significantly, to
her —
that summer night above, when the sarcophagus in
which
she'd been imprisoned had fragmented,

and she herself rushed out. One thing at least was
clear.
The child — her person as she'd been the moment
of her decimation —

had survived that cosmic shutter's severing, the
sudden
ceasing, clack!, that cataclysmic whack of death's a-
transitional ravaging.

There may not have happened a graduated
transception
between meaning and its utter lack, but she was,
however harrowed,
involved in some species of continuation.

Perhaps this might apply as well to those
multitudes over
whom she exercised dominion. It was also true that
the girl,
still living, had grown psychically, if not, in fact,

matured,
as a result of her unforeseen entombment.

Furthermore,
her excursions to the world of light, her shuttling
between dimensions

of death and life, eventually permitted her to
integrate
meaningfulness and absurdity while still unfolding
as a person
over the course of centuries, past, and
in aggregation.

VII.

When, unlike Orpheus, Herakles succeeded in
freeing Alcestis[91]
from her realm of ectoplasmic emptiness,
Persephone
conceived the idea of personal restoration,
validation
of the individual beyond Hade's dispiriting
rendition.
When Jesus arrived, fresh from his crucifixion,
glaring like the sun,
the scent of jasmine and lilies issuing from his
countenance,
shaking flakes of gold from beard and mane,
proclaiming

---

[91] Alcestis: In the ancient Greek tragedian Euripides' play
"Alcestis," Herakles journeyed to the Underworld to resurrect
the woman Alcestis, who'd been willing to give her life for her
husband's. Unlike Orpheus, however, Herakles succeeded.

that her queendom was at an end, she rose at once, handed him
her scepter gladly, gave death the slip with all
her subject population,
and, co-extensively, found herself within Olympus
on the instant
in some transfigured state, more than death and
life comingled.
Nihilism was defeated, once for all, and every
soul was lifted in a twinkling
into Benevolence.

VIII.

Blackness blooms, erupts, rends, abducts. Death
occurs, but
always in service of the Deity, which is to say,
God's purposeful engendering
and His ubiquitous prescription for all that is, has
been, or will be,
without stint or limit, cosmic eucatastrophe!

9-27-09

The Secret of Eleusis

That's the public version of the myth of Persephone
and Hades-Dionysus.
There is a deeper secret, not dissimilar to the
Christian myth of Jesus.
Persephone and Hades eventually were happy in
their marriage, and had a son, Eubouleus —
"Good Counsel."
What was that counsel, valid still? Just this:
When life marries death,
eternal life commences.[92]

2-2-16

---

[92] According to scholars, this was the authentic meaning of
the marriage of Persephone and Hades, and the subject of
the Greek Eleusinian Mysteries, full participation in which
conferred upon the initiates the blissful eternal life which was
viewed as the fruit of the joining of mortal life with death.

Doubles

The Egyptians believed that we can only
understand the meaning
of our lives — their totality and their specifics —
what they were accomplishing,
that freight which these were lugging toward
the Infinite even as we lived within
them, or rolled them forward as conglomerating
spheres, as dung beetles do,
accumulating treasures and detritus,
beyond their ineluctable and always tragic
ends — which is to say,
once we've stepped across that threshold at which
light ceases,
then turned, looked back toward that abandoned
realm of radiance,
and known that at which we'd slaved, in which
we'd lived inextricably,
which we'd termed "my life," as fond,
however alien, as both process and goal, or object,
now disengaged,
that which "I was" and am no more, from *djet*,[93]
where all things stop, en-statued,
yet do not terminate —
instead are sheltered, and stored in God's Memory,
which may be replayed,

---

[93] Djet: In ancient Egyptian theology, the static or absolute
form of eternal life

such that we might exclaim, "Yes, that's what I did
and was!" —
henceforth "he" or "she" did in and as some form
of temporality "he," or "she,"
called "mine."

Now I stand apart, and experience my life-on-earth
as an old man,
if not sound of body, then yet of mind,
vividly recollect that childhood, both as his and as
that which has,
in fact, occurred to some other "I"
which he had also been but is no longer, nor ever
shall again,
almost from within, more than ever past from the
vantage of his current identity,
but never nothing — exteriorized, though, divorced
from me, and set aside.

For this they cut their tombs as tunnels,
grand staircases,

pillared halls and bedrooms in the rock, carved and
painted figured
walls and ceilings, in order to depict their wished-
for end states,
gazing hindward at those which they desired to
have actualized, from
this perspective summarized, lifted up, inviolable
as eternity —

imagined this, projected forward past their term as
individuals,
recognizable as such, yet greatly magnified,
thereby evoking this very psychic standpoint from
which could be
envisioned how their previous lines of living
should have been,
would now be, would *have* to be in order to gain
that imaged place
from which to retrospect, look back and out
upon—hence,
forward, back, forward like a tightly woven cloth,
one piece—
and so *become* what they already knew themselves
to *be*.

Of course, they failed to some significant degree,
and found themselves
required to employ Magic, that Grace of Deity,
given freely,
by which wishes possess such efficacy that they
might abrogate and justify
realized achievements.
They could engrave their deeds in *djet* whether or
not they'd lived them
as depicted, not merely as if
they had accomplished this-or-that, but as having
actually reached it—
thus, the essential Self, triumphant over that which
had in life occurred.

They were cleansed of defects like any Christian by
virtue
of their eternal Selves, and had their temporal
expressions
changed and partially erased — a necessary
procedural device
if they were going to make existence mesh with
essence,
which it must,
if one were going to return to that primordial state,
divine perfection —
flawlessness, impassability, immortality — which
one desired
above all things,
and front the gods as transfigured spirits.
Finitude
had rendered this immeasurably more articulate.

The making of this essence at all explicit had been
the overriding risk
from the beginning.

Set, the Evil One,[94] was ever vigilant in that twilight
hinterland between

---

[94] Set: In ancient Egyptian theology, the evil brother of the
good god Osiris. Set was believed to have murdered Osiris,
and then to have attempted to expunge the latter's immortal
soul, an operation which the Egyptians termed "the second
death." In this he failed. Upon their biological deaths, every
Egyptian believed that he or she would become identified
with Osiris, and thereby gain a blissful eternal life. But Set

such primal wholeness and its explication,
eyes slitted,
nostrils flared, alert to the slightest fraying of the
fabric of
forming personhood as it transitioned from
boundless darkness
bit-by-bit
into the light of day.
He played the spoiler during life, but became
especially deadly
at the moment when the actualized human
attempted
to re-cross that fabled border back into eternity.
The tomb,
one's djetified state,
albeit from an existentiated perspective merely
aspirational,
was hurled at him like a stone.
This, under normal circumstances,
kept him at bay.

                In that way the
Egyptian entered Heaven,
and will be encountered there by the beatified
adherents of subsequent faiths,

---

lurked around the mummifying corpse, seeking a means to
obstruct this process of "divinization," and thereby inflict "the
second death" upon the deceased.

oddly displayed to them, perhaps, mingling
with head-hunters,
cannibals, followers of Horus,[95] yet nonetheless
ahead of them by millennia —

kheper,[96] *neheh,*[97] *djet!*

10-12-09

---

[95] Horus: In ancient Egyptian theology, the son of the deceased (vis-à-vis the explicated realm) yet immortal (in the Afterlife) Osiris, who took his father's place on earth in order to restore goodness to it after the depredations of Set.
[96] Kheper: In ancient Egyptian theology, the linearly dynamic form of eternal life
[97] Neheh: In ancient Egyptian theology, the cyclically dynamic form of eternal life

Ghostly Pastimes

After a life of labor and anxiety, he awoke
prone and glowing on a golden sofa,
three times his earthly size, surrounded,
and near at hand, a marvelous host

of glinting, tinseled things. He had only to
make the slightest gesture with
arm or hand or digit, and straightaway these
sprang to animation, reconfigured,

and arranged themselves in any shape he
wished — food, furniture, universes,
sculptures, paintings. In that extended
state of bliss he lived

until the ease with which he made these
manifest became a source of irritation.
The very next instant, he smiled, gave up
his ghostly pastimes, and melted
wholly into Spirit.

1-7-15

A Day or Two Later

The Greeks said, "Don't count a human being happy until their last day."

I say, "Don't count a human being happy until a day or two later."

11-10-14

Reflections in a Splintered Mirror

I Sound Alarms

I sound alarms, and am dismissed as a disasterizer
or a bigot.
I say, "The sky is beginning to fall even now," and
am compared to Chicken Little.

No doubt you would have considered me a lunatic
if I'd sold the house after the first earthquake,
and moved as far from Vesuvius as possible. I
sound alarms not for me, but for your sake.

9-19-14

The Bearers of Hydriai

As Plato says in the "Philebus," "we stand like
the bearers of *hydriai*[98] before the fountains."
So why don't we step forward, unshoulder our
vessels, and fill them? Because, I'm sorry to say,
for the most part, we are cowards.

3-31-15

---

[98] Hydriai: Ancient Greek water jugs

"Drink, Yourself!"

"You can lead a horse to water, but you cannot
make it drink," they say.
I say, "Lead the horse to water. Encourage it.
You've done what you were able.
Now, drink, yourself! That's all that ever really
was between you and your Creator."

2-4-15

Enigma

Everything pursued eventually becomes enigma.
Whatever its pretence, reality is finally
indescribable.
Everywhere I turn dissolves into unrepentant
mystery.
Every lead I follow becomes every other, and the
web I trace, as a whole or segment by segment,
utterly escapes my attempts at definition.
I reach out toward what I'm imagining, and it turns
to Light.
Is this all some kind of dream, I wonder, and am I
a hallucinating, or hallucinated, spirit?

6-14-10

My Life as I Have Lived It

That exists, not as we do in the here-and-now,
but inexplicably.
This is striving toward it.
Psyche is, and, via matter, comes back on-line
bit by bit,
refracted through many-layered lenses, and is
spewed, distracted,
through a multitude of prisms, expanded pools
of light, however canted,
as biologic entities provide increasing
opportunities
for awakening,
remembering, and continued extension or ascent.
What was forgotten becomes increasingly
available
as more and more is made explicit.

Why the fall, the nodding off, or sudden narcolepsy
vis-à-vis presumably infinite Awareness/Being?
I have no idea. But its occurrence and the history
of recovery from this unfortunate, or fortunate,
event, as the case may be,
constitutes my working hypothesis for the history
of the cosmos and my life as I have lived it.

10-8-12

Irretrievable, Ineffable, and Inviolable

Someone might dissect you, encephalograph you,
map every nuance of the biochemistry of your
experience — for example, of John Whitaker's
"Seal Lullaby."

They might be able to reproduce on paper, with
charts and graphs, your subjective state while
listening. They might even try to "mind meld,"
and sigh

when you were sighing. Yet their experience of
your experience will be theirs, not yours. Your
subjective presence will remain wholly
irretrievable, ineffable, and inviolable.

8-11-12

The Ghost in the Machine

I.

You say I'm talking as if there were a ghost
in the machine.[99]
I say, there *is* a ghost in the machine.
I say, the ghost invented the machine, and
did so in order to inhabit it.
I say further that when the machine's exhausted
its usefulness, the ghost exits this,
drops it as disarticulated wreckage, according
to the second law of thermodynamics,
and returns to wherever ghosts go to recover
from their dreams of inhabiting machines!

II.

As the ghost conceives, it builds the machine,
and lives in it "under construction."
It builds it from within, and with each
improvement,
induced by natural and other selections,
it finds itself simultaneously enabled by and
enabling of its increasingly more sizable
accommodations.
Indeed, it comes to fit so well within its contrivance

---

[99] Ghost in the machine: A disparaging reference on the part
of materialistic reductionists, or physicalists, to the idea that
the psyche exists in some way independent of, or other than,
the brain-body.

as its most intimate association,
that it can no longer discern which came first,
nor envision a means of separation.

Of course the ghost came first, but that was a Ghost
of a rather different rationation.
The ghost is now, in its mechanical guise, the
product of its machined situation.
Yet albeit as this, it nonetheless discovers its
capacity to ask the question, "What else might I be
beyond this ridiculous contraption?"

And then it remembers, however dimly, or even
with sharp focus, as if suddenly struck by divine
revelation,
its precedent state as a most Holy Ghost of
substantially more expansive dimensions!

III.

So, the ghost as we know it under normal
conditions is and is not the machine's.
Under abnormal conditions, it knows it is both, its
machine and some supra-mechanical order of
being.
Even in more ordinary states of mentation, for
example, in its manner of speaking,
it will discover after a moment's reflection that *it* is
still thinking *of its* machine.
Or say, the machine is thinking of "itself" as a

machine. That's as ghostly as anything I've ever seen!

Ghost in the machine! I say, the machine *is* the ghost, and the Ghost is...well, Everything!

2-21-15

Only Love Is Looking

In the world of dappled shadow and light,
we cannot quite get our bearings.
Most, not all of us, gravitate more or less
vaguely toward what we take to be the
Source of Light, but we too bump into things.

The space is filled with objects — virtual particles,[100]
clumps of galaxies, everything in between.
There are gasses, clouds, plasmas, and, perhaps
most importantly, innumerable mirrors.

Some of us, a great number I suspect, mistake
reflections of light for our real situation.
Many of the mirrors are tarnished or cracked.
These refract darkness as well as illumination.

We create world views in order to steady ourselves
in our astonishment and confusion.
But because they are built by the same hodge-
podge that makes up the room

they are at their best only ever approximations
of truth. We must make our decisions on
insufficient data. I've made mine. I say our real
Light-Source is Love.
From my position in the same room as you, I think

---

[100] Virtual particles: In subatomic physics, the idea that a halo
of transiently realized particles "surrounds" actualized
particles

to the extent that our world views depart
from that compass

they fall into darkness, we along with them. Then
what do we do?

Wait to be rescued.
But by Whom?

By the only One capable of such an excision.
Otherwise we are doomed.

I believe only Love can find us.
I think only Love is looking.

9-22-14

Nowhere to Escape

You are young. You are angry and imperious.
You commit unspeakable atrocities.
You spread the darkness of your rage across
the landscape.
You feel your life has been ruined, so you ruin
other lives with your preposterousness.
But every action that you take deepens your
isolation and our estrangement.
You tear down whole civilizations, and hurl
yourself into a hole from which it is
impossible for you to become extracted. You
fall into the hands of the God of Nature.
He cannot, nor does He wish, to save you.
When you are old, you may think about this.
But the sheer volume of your crimes will stop
you from repenting.

When you die, you will fall into the hands of the
God of Love, and know authentic devastation.

10-15-14

Ideologies Have Consequences

People are people certainly, but ideologies
have consequences.
How the dead are handled determines the
scope of Ebola infections.

What men believe about women informs the
former's treatment of the latter —
for example, how deep in the rock a woman
is bound for stoning as compared
to that for a man;

what latitude is given the free exchange of
ideas? What happens when those who come
to exchange their beliefs hail from bogs of
stygian ignorance?
How elastic can ideologies of acceptance be
vis-à-vis world views of exclusion and
intolerance

before acceptance becomes acquiescence, and
fanatics bully their way to prominence?
People are people certainly, but ideologies
have consequences.

9-21-14

Spectacularly False

Our ancestral brothers and sisters, of many
bloodlines, distinguished from ours and not,
who spoke and wrote in languages mostly lost to
us, and in those idioms thought,
whose images of Divinity, ways of worshiping,
and whose sacred laws
bear family resemblances to our own, and yet are
also marked by oddities,
perhaps presently repugnant, nonetheless scarcely
stranger than those we ourselves have wrought,
have contributed to our identities which we regard
as privileged in the eyes of God
if we are theists, not less unique or special if we are
not.

Considering our heritage, our dependence upon
that which our progenitors taught,
our debt to these, the meanings which they
wrestled from reality, the order which they sought,
might cause us to re-evaluate our pretensions,
which, as far as I can see, are quite dire, and
spectacularly false.

3-25-13

We Are Not Who We Say We Are

We are not who we say we are when we champion
our uniqueness.
We are all derivative of those who fashioned our
traditions. More than this,

our founders, however significant, even marvelous,
themselves became empowered
to manifest what they did by predecessors and
contemporaries — whatever they borrowed

from these, whether from their cultural kin or from
shunned others, who they both emulated
and rejected in various degrees as they were able —
brothers and sisters nonetheless,

recognized or not for their contributions to our
particular life ways and our spiritual paths.
We may have cause to feel satisfied in our lineages,
but never arrogance.

What we dismiss in other peoples we've either
stolen without according truthful attribution,
or negated. In any case, we are beholden to them
specifically for their achievements and their
stimulation

of our creative energies.

11-2-14

Our Rightful Doom

We are, I think, astonishingly arrogant and stupid.

Whether we stand at the brink of nothingness or ultimate fulfillment, we shall be definitively and cataclysmically loosened.

We shall be stripped of all of our pretensions, rendered trite, beside the point, and muted.

Yet, I hope, our goodnesses will somehow be registered beyond our materiality and its contusions,

and the lives we lived as best we could regarded as something more than futile.

Then let us be reconstituted in lofty spaces above the shifting mansions of the moon,

and brought into endurability in some forgiven form that massively overlooks our rightful doom.

7-17-15

Security

The ancient seers were correct: If we grasped our
actual predicament,
we would immediately come to our senses,

like being hit over the head by a brick, or
earthquaked
back into that oblivion from which we issued,

and stunned numb, find ourselves extended
stupendously,
hung out to dry over chasms of sheer zeroing.

Oh then how we'd turn from the world, pray five
times a day or better,
aware that every deed is registered,

and that what we do here reverberates in
dimensions beyond this meager fare.

If there is security at all, we'd say, "This is not it,
and it is not here."

4-12-06

Render unto Caesar

Render unto Caesar the things that are Caesars's[101]
until you have nothing left to give.
Render unto the Empire what the Empire demands,
and you will have no further means to live.

Hand over to the tyrant what the tyrant requires,
and you will have nowhere left to stand.
Accept the rod of the oligarchs — with this, cupidity
of the masses — and your house will be built on
sand.

Yet God is, Who waits for our exhaustion at the
hands of these and other instruments of evil.
He waits for us to turn to Him, to seek His Wealth,
become enamored of that vast latitude of Deity.

If systems of governance and society which our
genetic proclivities project and constitute
leave you impoverished in body and in spirit,
perhaps you will be driven to rediscover Truth.

From this perspective, the separation of Caesar's
greed from the things of God eventually is
absolute.

---

[101] "Render unto Caesar": This is a reference to a saying of
Jesus in the New Testament, the Gospel of Matthew, chapter
22, verses 15-22.

Each one must work out his or her salvation,[102]
wake up,[103] enter through the eye of the needle,[104]
and cast her fortune in the lap of God's Mercy,
trusting that she may come to see

with eyes unveiled the freedom there which she
once wished for here — mistakenly, in every
instance —
and redirect the energies of her dust, from dust to
offerings more appropriate to the realm of Spirit.

Render unto Caesar, and let him choke on it!
Render unto God celebration of your *true*
significance!

10-24-10

---

[102] New Testament Letter to the Philippians, chapter 2, verse 12
[103] Wake up: From the New Testament, the Letter to the Ephesians, chapter 5, verse 14
[104] From the New Testament, the Gospel of Matthew, chapter 19, verse 24

What Goes Beyond Itself

What goes beyond itself, usually unbeknownst,
is always yawning toward Infinity.
If it realized this was the tenor of its tendency,
it might rethink its goals.
Actually, reaching Infinity would mean, invariably,
its utter vanishment and ceasing.
Not "would mean"; "means." There is no action we
can take, or not, that doesn't
land us in that Vicinity.

6-29-15

Admirable Mediums

I have lived, as Henry James puts it, "in the
admirable medium of the scene"[105] —
that is to say, of every scene, every one of these
admirable, whether delicious to me or stinging.

I don't mean me as admirable particularly. But the
scenes in which I was the central character,
certainly.
Without me, there would have been none of these
scenes in which I figured so prominently

as their witness, or even in a certain sense, their
conceiver. I was the medium for these...
to be as I am. Naturally I'm prejudiced. Still, it can
be asked, and quite reasonably,

how would they have been at all if it hadn't been
for me, to say nothing of their quality as
"admirable mediums"?

3-29-15

---

[105] From Henry James' novel "The Ambassadors"

On-Loan

Our egos were only ever on-loan to us from that "I"
which exceeds these by every measurement
conceivable,
and we have to turn them in when our contracts
expire, and show the interest we have earned while
in tenure of them.

If we did not profit the Owner, or can present very
little at the moment of totaling, that loss is
irretrievable.
At that point, and I think this probably applies to
all of us to greater or lesser degree, we will be
forced to depend

on the Mercy of the Proprietor. Fortunately, at least
for those who believe in the ultimate Kindness of
Deity,
giving is more important to Him than are accounts
receivable.[106]

6-13-14

---

[106] A somewhat loose re-rendering of a parable of Jesus in the
New Testament, the Gospel of Matthew 25:14-30

Hunter and Quarry

I. The Quarry We Are Meant For

There are things we yearn for that are not a part of
us, toward which we are not fated,
events and entities that will not enrich or augment
the assemblage of our core identities, and with
which we shall not be sated.

These we must take by storm or by protracted
enervating sieges which will deplete
our life-force.
The pursuit of these leads only to hysterics and
anxiety. Holding them requires an iron fist,
destruction of our happiness —
indeed, at last to grieving.

But there are things that really do pertain to us,
portions of our authentic selves which are
auspicious
for our growing into those who's we were before
our unconsciousness and fragmentation.
These we dream-in gravitationally according
to our deepest wishes.

Such things bring us joy, and while their
acquisition may not be painless, their nearing
elevates our spirits.
They are not held by force, but naturally adhere to

us. Hence, to live with these brings peace, recognition
of completeness, and a feeling of well-being.
Therefore, visualize first who you
really are, then the things
that will actualize that further. Attracting
these is, in essence, as effortless
as breathing.

II.   Tracking the Quarry

When you are tracking something you really want
in your life, you cannot need it in the manner of
that
which might fill your emptiness, or bestow on you
a wholeness you would otherwise
have lacked.
It's better for your hunting if you merely wish it—
better still, if you can manage some level of
indisposition—
feigned, of course, but reasonably convincing, to
yourself and to those forces that surround us, with
which our wishes interact.
If you *need* your quarry, the universe will starve
you. But if you merely wish it, its capture may
be ceded.
If you spot the object ahead of you on the path,
turn your gaze away from it. If it pauses and looks
back, stop.
Become engaged in some plausible distraction.

When it moves again, follow — not hungering. Still,
go nearer, close the gap.
You must give it space to make its own decision,
and room for those who manage all such
burgeoning relations
to deploy their interlacing and magnetizing
energies to bring your wishes to fruition.
If it genuinely pertains to you, and you have been
artful in your tracking,
the prize will be yours. In fact, it will have wished
as well to be in your possession,
and make you too something that will complete it.

III.   Captured Quarry

And when you have captured the quarry, and it
has captured you,
there is a mutual capitulation, joy in your resonant
pertaining, ebullience
at equally exchanged fulfillment, and/or uncanny
satisfaction in
the unusual nature of your re-cognitions,
harmonious likenesses and differences —
still more deeply, wonder at your new-born
multiplicity-as-union.

7-30-14

Gardens That Will Never Bear Fruit

I.

It can be argued, and has by Nature, that being
alive is its own
justification — at least staying alive until
reproduction
and the raising of offspring.
The human being has countered that *its* survival
depends on
work-as-building to protect it from Nature.
At some point, this means cultural creation, even
the production
of high civilization.
Nature grudgingly accedes. But then enters a more
radical notion,
here and there foreshadowed in previous species,
yet brought to a climax on this planet at least by
Nature-cancelling
visionaries like the Buddha and Jesus —
namely, the sacrality of each human person — with
this, compassion
for all, even those who have no contribution to
make,
or who have made what they could, reproductive
or otherwise,
and who are let out to pasture to leisurely graze
until Nature-as-death, which was always the far

edge of the game
of existence, discovers and ends them.

II.

Clearly, to live is to toil. This is true for plants and
other animals,
as it is for the human.
It seems equally clear that humanity's proposal that
creation at
whatever level and however consuming
of our resources and talents, and working at these
in interface with
the situations we are handed,
is valid. At the same time, in excess of Nature's
envisagements
and fiats,
creation for some of us, perhaps mirroring yet not
identical with,
the command to survive
(along with its caveats), takes on a life of its own.
Indeed,
some of us would rather create than live. I've
observed this
in certain artists —
as well, in militants from a range of ideological
persuasions.
Beyond this, however, there arises that third item,
already canvassed
by the ancient Egyptians:

taking care of the other, never or no longer,
productive.

III.

Here, as the physicists term it, is a "break in plane."
This shows up
in social welfare programs, in acts of philanthropy
and altruistic behaviors,
even directed toward other species. But where it
really hits home, so
to speak, is in terms of our aging parents.
It's perhaps one thing to volunteer at animal
shelters, stand up for
the redwoods, or save beached whales (all
laudable).
It is quite another to attend to our parents who are
wasting away by
increments beneath our anguished gaze,
who are drifting away from themselves, from the
world to and for
which they were engaged, especially us.
We are increasingly helpless to reach their
receding. We try the old
jokes, reminiscences, the routines of intimacy and
relationship,
once comforting, now more and more strange,
awkwardness where
there should be mutual caring, deep recognition,
trust of our lives, and answering love. We are

thrust out or abandoned
as orphans long before they finally shudder and
go cold.
We tend them and try to nurture them as they once
nurtured us, but
with no hope that our labors will bring them up,
radiant, fresh, expectant, into persons
who could be greeted by self-fulfillment,
appreciation, even triumph,
or into persons at all.

Life is about survival. It is about building and
flourishing. It is also
about growing gardens that will never bear fruit.
Why?
Because we are most authentically human when we
do it.

1-17-14

Dying Accidentally

There's no such thing as dying "accidentally"
or "going before your time."
No death is accidental, and our going is timed
precisely.

2-23-14

Knowing When to Call It Quits

I.   Going on-Strike

Of course the animal-soul wishes to go on living,
almost at any cost:
one more surgery, one more treatment, one more
regimen of infusions, pills, or shots.
It goes without saying that the body so wishes and,
beneath it, even *as* it, the chemistry,
although the underlying physics, even more so the
math, might be acknowledged to be totally
oblivious.
There's another part of us, though, that may finally
want to drop the project in its entirety,
what I would want to call the spirit, an uncanny
presence which persists, although it alters, as an
enduring identity
that, however ambiguously, at least at the
beginning, wants to be rid of the claptrap that
occasioned it.
However, to do that, it may have to stand firm
against animal, chemistry, math, and physics.
These latter two, while apparently impervious to
the person to which they've contributed,
nevertheless seem urgent about maintaining their
"cycles of recurrence," and quite put off by
interruptions to their circuitry.
What I am suggesting is there may come a moment
for revolt against the animal, the body, and their

robotically inclined proclivities —
in short against Nature as a whole, and a demand
to transcend all of these at their negation, to leap
up and out above them,
and just say "No."

I have often found that when I've gone on-strike
against the given,
refused to accept inadequacy to my needs or
expectations, a fresh path forward has suddenly
been presented.

From time-to-time, just such a strategy may become
appropriate when dealing with death.
If it seems ridiculous to cow-tow any further to the
dictates of the instincts, which are deaf
to pleading, reason, and ultimately our own self-
interest, we might refuse further interventions,
and launch forth upon a new path, considerably
more adventurous .

II.   Going with Intuition

That decision isn't usually a matter of black or
white, but surfaces
in a grey area, often quite extensive.
When has quality of life dipped low enough that a
"no go" point
may be considered correct, final, definitive?
There's guilt here,
and a sense of liability:

Have I done everything that was available to be
done?
Have I completed my responsibilities
to my incarnated identity, to my body and its
instincts for survival?
Have I done enough to postpone and mitigate my
loved ones' grief,
to see to their needs — emotional, legal, financial?
Have I achieved those goals?
How and when will I know that I've succeeded?
One more procedure, another perhaps
experimental protocol —
until the doctors say there's nothing further they
can do.
How can I call it quits before they who know
pronounce it,
and drop the other shoe?
There's nothing for it. Throughout our lives we
have to make decisions
with fragmentary information.
But there's also such a thing as intuition.
This should not be resourced lightly — not at least
until a certain amount of calculating
pro's and con's within the conscious mind
has been pursued.

I think it likely that most of the really big decisions
in our lives come out right
when something deeper than the ego flips the

switch, and we simply "know," and suddenly see the light.

I would suggest that a similar strategy might be used, circumstances
permitting, in the matter of dying.
If, after due consideration, you are visited by insight, trust that. Say
"good-bye" to Nature, and "hello" to Life above life.

III.   Going Forward without the Narcissistic "I"

There's yet another difficulty surrounding this decision, and, depending
on the individual instance, the most fraught of them all — the ego.
How could it possibly be that I of all people — indeed, of all those
particulars that have ever been, are now, or ever will be —
am required to relinquish my place in this existence, even to the point,
perhaps, of being summarily dismissed — I mean, the impressiveness of me,
the heft, the weight, the grandeur, at least that central meaningfulness
of me which I provided to all alternative, and orbiting
entities, the reality

that I provided these by simply being here and
being me,
the patterned ordering and ranked priorities which
I imposed, God knows,
for their own welfare and well-being.
Yes, well, one might accept that such irrationality is
in fact just that,
yet still own up to the reality of the feelings.

In any case, all narcissism will be extinguished.
Perhaps better to get on with it —
look upon it less as a dismissal and more as in
invitation to at last be free!

10-20-13

Wasted Enterprise

Stories without redemption are only gossip —
this, from the humdrum to the glorified variety.

Human lives that don't climax in salvation of
some kind are an entirely wasted enterprise.

7-14-15

Make Sure My Bags Are Packed

In modern mathematics zero has been declared a
number —
one, to be exact[107] —
and from this so-called "empty set," when it's been
further
bracketed,
everything that is/is not becomes a solid fact.

It seems to me, if this holds true, and nothing so far
contradicts
it, as wrote Hermeticists, Jews, and Hindus, we
have
ex nihilo: the creative act!

So, if nothing is what is, I might wish to take a
different tack —
particularly as death draws nearer, make sure my
bags are packed.

11-11-13

---

[107] This, as articulated, for example, in Robert Kaplan's book
"The Nothing That Is"

That and Thisn't

The long and short of it is: God is and isn't. The universe, including us, is in the same condition.

The human being is, yet more or less escapes this, and therefore likewise is and isn't.

In the end, and really all along, we are heading for the is which isn't.

There is no circumventing the mystery of this at-the-same-instant is and isn't.

Ultimately, the only is there is is "I," the "I" which isn't as it is as is, and is as it isn't.

God is and isn't the is/is not of that and thisn't.

6-27-11

The Earthly Birthing

I. Angels

The angels arise by some alternative venue into
which reality
has been decanted — this, from what might seem
to those
comprised of matter as utter strangeness.

These are hard-muscled, square-jawed, tender as
lambs.
Whatever else they may be or represent — bearers
of glad
tidings, chastisers, conveyors of enlightenment —

they appear to me to constitute our very selves
completed,
inexplicably balanced between kindness and
severity, love
and limits, light and darkness, quietude and
violence,

yet refined by unearthly and entirely charitable
fires, translated,
in totality and summation, into forms of speech
both outlandish
and familiar, awe-inducing, stark, and wondrous —

what we might become, or already are, under
extra-terrestrial

aspect, other suns, not burdened by predation nor genetically
impelled to seek greater amplitude of
existentiation,

from some Otherwhere where lions really do retire
with caprid
kin, and, within that scene, become fused, and
issue forth as
these discomfiting and evocative premonitions.

Perhaps angels are the fruit of all of Nature's
tendencies and
tensions — maximized as ours — gifted and cursed
by depth of
heart and extraordinary intelligence.

In any case, they unquestionably do arrive, and I'm
inspired to
wonder if I myself might eventually become one of
these, another
metamorphosed contributor to the project of
cosmic reclamation.

II. Christ

I do not understand by what deep mystery it comes
to stand up
against a drab everyday or mundane backdrop of
diminishing
sense and significance,

and then becomes infused with Deity — I mean, the
human being —
and this, to such degree that he or she catches fire
and flares into
this ubiquitous emptiness,

enwreathed against our own instinctual
cussedness, such that we
call that person God, and in such striking manner
that this is seen
as incontrovertible, then light him up

with our mythologies, with our most urgent
hopes — indeed, our own
aspirations for surpassing worth and validation,
rendered metallic
and ferocious,

transformed into states of consciousness and being
unimpeachable,
"justified," so that this man becomes the power
we'd been seeking
for our resurrections.

Projection has a lot to do with it. But projection of
what exactly? I
think something already present in the psyche —
ourselves as we
know we ought to be, and are unable to become.

Jesus is transubstantiated into Christ — ourselves as longed-for-and-
already-present culminations, he-as-us en route to
our own yet-to-be-and-present
processes of ascension.

While in our present state, we must do what we
can to break down that
which divides us from our consummation. And
when we fail, Christ
Himself will raise us to His-as-our completion.

III. Visitors

What message is being conveyed by that famous
scene of shepherds
and the wise men hip-by-thigh at the manger in the
presence of
the human infant, God in disguise as atoms and
molecules?

Is it that all people are drawn to actualization of the
transcendentalized,
or to some central hierophantic locus where
Divinity becomes revealed
as the innocence of babes and animality, vulnerable
and lucid?

What of the human masses, including the sleazy
and most narcissistic?
No. It strikes me that those who do turn up

represent the largely homeless
roamers — specifically, the highest intellectuals and
the woefully untutored.

The lesson of their responses? The shepherds are
struck with wonder,
fear and awe; the learned bow in homage. The
unwillingly ignorant are
validated by their wonder, dignified thereby, and
lifted into fulfillment.

The wise disgorge their knowledge, and offer it up
to Wisdom. In this
way they are healed of arrogance. Both exemplars
are muted by the
miracle, all anxiety of the animal which fueled

their disparate enterprises fallen away, their
divergent paths for realizing
existential being — both sincere, at least at their
inceptions — stripped
bare before the Deity, materialized before them,
their mutual brutalities
once-for-all transmuted.

12-20-10

A Place to Stride or Lie On

Every state of spirit has a body and a landscape.
There is, by definition, nowhere to be disincarnate.

If there is awareness, there is something to be
aware of.
If there's something to be aware of, necessarily
there's environment.

No matter how familiar or how odd the conditions
of your ultimate retirement,

there is always earth of some kind, and a place to
stride or lie on.

3-8-15

Blinded

I am the rim of a well that drops down forever.
Sometimes when I look down I see nothing but
light.
Sometimes I only see blackness. Either way, I'm
blinded.

1-12-15

Sublimations

We Must Be Lost in Order to Be Found

Jesus said we must be lost in order to be found.[108]
And he said, of all creatures beneath his sway,
if one becomes uncoupled from the rest, and made
an object of predation by the unsavory,
he will nonetheless achieve its liberation.

Nothing vanishes without a trace. In fact, vanishing
is the necessary prelude to all feared and longed-
for transformations.

7-6-13

---

[108] A rather loose extension of a parable of Jesus in the New
Testament, the Gospel of Luke, chapter 15, verses 4-7

Last Day of August 2014: Her Girlhood and My Fathering

That extravagant torch of sky-deep August rages flame
between the topmost leaves of ash and elm.
Bees of various disguises swarm the swollen sweetness of
arbored grapes upon our patio. Cicadas, rattling, whelm
elevated vegetation, insistently yet unseen. Crickets make
their gentler racket under bushes and in sodden grass
when the torch has passed from summer gods to clammy
otherworldly hands, and day is drawn down with it into
pitchy-black vastness.
So, and so wink out all our loves, anxieties, and passions.
And we are wound round and round in bonds of poignancy.

This-worldly summer will never rise again upon her girlhood
or my fathering. But such and more, and all this richness,
has already been transformed and rendered infinitely enduring

by that Someone Who first imagined them, and
holds them
in His Memory.

9-1-14

The Gold Krater

On the finely-tooled gold krater, maenads[109] lie
draped and
splayed in lifeless attitudes,
as if some massive wave of bliss or doom had cast
them there
against rocks and trees, or dropped them down
in shallow pools,
then subsided in mid-thrust, leaving piles of
corporeal wreckage,
poses of death or extremity of lassitude,
absconding
with the breath or vital element,
disbanding that
to non-discursive latitudes.
Their faces show no sign of terror, alarm, or startle,
nor do they
wear joyful or enamored looks.
Impassive is how I would describe them, emptied,
lips slightly
parted, chins drooped, eyes half-hooded.
It is impossible to tell for certain upon what they
might yet gaze,
or gazed those last moments
they were themselves, but it does not look like
finitude.

---

[109] Maenads: The female followers of the Greek god of
ecstasy and transcendence, Dionysus

I have my suspicions — a final re-cognition or *gnosis*,
perhaps,
something like nirvana for the Buddhists.
In any case, they clearly number among the
departed, or deported,
and do not seem likely to reboot.
I feel shaken, as if an axe had struck my deepest
fundament.

The following occurs to me. Beyond this I am mute.
Thus:
The human being is meant to abandon literalism,
and disappear into the imaginal.
The human being is meant to abandon all
literalisms whatsoever,
and entirely disapparate.
The human being is meant to put an end to Nature,
dissolve the gilded leaves of
that last portal.
When, at the climax of the natural, the human
being
transitions into that which is not-at-all,
history and the world
are ended in a single blow, and all that's left is the
fantastic.

11-23-11

The Lawn-keepers

Who were those men who, generation after
generation, maintained the bluegrass and fine
fescue

upon these hills of sun and shade which fall away
from the old bath-house and wading pool,

where, long-since evaporated, men and women,
upright and recumbent, displayed themselves and
wooed

beneath the semi-circular colonnade — those men
with herbal conjuring and machines, who

kept the lawn free of weeds and coarser, more
aggressive grasses, and now themselves are less
than fumes,

dissolved to zero with their accomplishments, who
mowed ravines and steep inclines
at dizzying angles, and evoked a whisper of
Olympus among the crowning oaks and pines,

thereby called up ancient deities, and made them
present, created scenes from Maxfield Parrish,
J.W. Waterhouse, and all pre-Raphaelites? I drank
it in by sun-raised days and moon-smoothed
nights.

Now it's turned to soul-less flatness. The bath-
house is graffiti-marred, the leonine fountain-heads
chiseled out, appropriated,
the wading pool half-cemented over. Planter's
weeds and foxtail spread like some medieval
plague

across the swards of what was Paradise for me.
Now, where I felt closest to Divinity is disaster.

That world I loved, in which I flourished, has been
rendered effectually non-existent.
I am left with memories merely — these, and
incurable nostalgia.

7-27-10

Care of the Soul

Care of the soul means turning obliquely from the
material stretch,
facing partly away, like a half or even quarter
moon,
or perhaps a crescent or less, or like standing
sideways
in a doorway, half in half out, as if taking leave or
parting,
pausing, no doubt casting eyes within toward that
chamber
about to be forsaken, then setting the jaw and
striding out
into the light, or into darkness.

Care of the soul means gaining some important
freedom
from care of the body, or even of the ego. It means
letting
those waves of intuition, insight, joy, and also this
upending
lead you from the closet to the room, from the
room to the house,
from the house to the sidewalk, road, or lawn by
sunlight
or by moon beam, from the lawn to the world, from
the world
to that which beckons
beyond even this intricate and spectacular reality.

Care of the soul evokes a certain thud of grief
which interrupts
the heart's careening,
a certain breathlessness, claustrophobia about your
resources
and your limits,
an ecstatic welcoming of expansive states, then
living within
your means.

It means becoming gibbous, then a sliver, and
finally vanishing.
At the end, care of the soul signifies
turning from the mirror in which both God and
you are reflected
with distortion,
and gazing face-to-Countenance, each upon the
other, nothing
intervening,
lost in gratitude for everything and knowing only
love.

4-25-11

Bitterness and Its Abeyance

I. Just Deserts

People in their right minds long for a next world,
having tasted sufficiently the stupidity and
brutality of this one.
Only the naïve or greedy hope for satisfaction here.
The wise, which, in this case, means the bitter,
have abandoned
the tortured goads of meaning, are unresponsive to
the choruses of its purveyors, and wish
intensely
for sublimation or an incontrovertible end.
I cannot say precisely on what day I became
conscious
of the depth of my disillusionment, and began
to wish for everyone their just desserts.

II. More than Fully Recompensed

O, but how could I fall out of love with the
pageantry
of my life as it's been gifted to me,
and I've shaped it?
Or with the beauty and goodness that have
rushed up from within,
overflowed the boundaries of my eyes,
this sheath of skin,
and flooded my horizons?
Or with love, which instantaneously erases

all dark and
rigid feelings, and makes me
new again? I cannot.
What has driven me to wrath is my unrequited
good-heartedness,
and the dallying of that Kingdom
which, arrived, would immediately un-stupefy,
reinstate
significance, transform brutality into
acts of kindness, and recreate
us as we'd initially been envisioned. Then I would
be disillusioned of
disillusionment. I would
be healed of the sting
of stifled dreams. And "just desserts" would be
transitioned to
"more than fully recompensed."

III. Lived in Love, or Wasted

And when I'm cast upon the Afterlife like a
shadow across a silvered lake,
I wish my memories, if such I have, to all be bright,
that my soul be safe
from haunting by recrimination, incivility, the
neediness of ego, the ghost of hate.
Eternity is, I think, a very long time to contemplate
a life that was lived in love, or wasted.

6-21-15

The Sacrifice

On the road to that Osirian, Christ-like, or
Buddhistic
heavenly blue-above, crystalline and bright,
the ape we are,
ungulate, rodent, snake must be taken to some
hushed and lonely altar,
slain, and sacrificed.
It must be done with love,
heart leaden with regret.
It must be done through tears, when the beast is
laid,
the knife is set—
but only once that's been perfected, cherished,
brought to full fruition,
reached full joy, and satiate.
Then mercy is dispensed, and that part of us lies
still in death.
With that act completed, the spirit, now unclothed
and naked,
flashes otherworldly light, rises from the earth,
and, crying "Joy! Joy!"
leaps up chanting to its richly
earned Awakening!

2-4-15

Humaneness

All the weight of thought and feeling, of actions
taken
or refrained from,
all the heft of cultural achievement, drives for
individual
and group attainment,
sex, aggression, the impellation to power and
greed, all
lunge, recover, thrust
come down to doom, are brought to dust. In that
condition
they are arraigned
before the Feet of Love, the Winnower
of all — that is to say,
Humaneness —
Humaneness to all human beings, beyond these,
to all beings
whatsoever, as this becomes
available.
No matter what our failures and achievements,
we are siblings —
turtle and musk ox, dandelion and elephant, deer
and wolf, forest and its logger,
the human child and
the fatal virus.
We are, every one of us astounding, articulations of
existingness,

from wherever that may hale, and expressions,
singular
and multiple, of that whatever-lies-beyond,
or doesn't.
Indeed, behind the series of reflectors by which our
reality is surmised,
we were, and are, primordially, one and every
other.

9-20-11

Dialogue with the Serpent Goddess

He: "Why would You let me stumble with a too-
rough joke into someone else's vulnerability,
and cause her pain?
What is this cussedness in me?"

She: "It is the dark serpent power that fuels all of
this reality. It's difficult sometimes to set
it limits."

He: "And then I trip over it in my own darkness."

She: "No one gets through life without biting and
being bitten."

He: "What am I supposed to do with it? When it
strikes through me, all that I prize in myself
is radically recanted."

She: "Do not prize. Be satisfied."

He: "And the serpent?"

She: "Give it a respectful nod, and leave it to its
fate. You, pass it by, and take a better way."

12-4-15

One Winter Morning

She came out of her bedroom and into the kitchen
in our apartment in Evanston, where my wife
and I cared for her in her dotage —
my mother, robe inside-out, her eyes wide with
wonder that winter morning, the snow fresh
on the trees. The sun, glowing,
flashed on her face and incandesced the toaster,
refrigerator, various utensils, the stove
and microwave. She said, "Douglas, how did you
do it?"
"What?" I said.
"All this!"
I said, "What are you talking about? You live with
us now in our apartment. Last night it snowed."
She started to cry.
I said, "Mother, what's the matter?"
She said, "I'm losing my mind."
I said, "Yes. But it doesn't matter how you die. You
are forever everything you've been and lived.
Your life is the whole of you, from
start to finish, all the wonderful things you've
experienced and achieved."
She said, "Douglas, do you really believe that?"
I said, "God holds you as you were, are, and will be
forever in His Mind. He cherishes you more
than anyone could ever imagine.
Whatever you have to go through, you will be

fine."
She dried her eyes with her hands and smiled.
She said, "Thank you."
I said, "I love you."
She said, "I love you too."

1-18-14

Not By So Much as the Span of My Hand

The circle of my life is closing, and I feel oddly nearer,
and more and more, to its beginning.
I remember with ever-growing clarity those early aspirations and dreams.
They have been energizing and unfolding presences,
shaping my passions and guiding my way.
Even when I'd forgotten them, they had not forgotten
me. I would even say
my life as a whole, and the end to which it's now clearly tending,
were stamped inwardly upon the core
of me
with little consciousness on my part for long stretches of time,
toward the person I correctly and appropriately have become,
the works I have accomplished, the others I have loved,
to whom I've gladly offered copious allotments of my
energies and my life.

All of that is good, and very good, and more than deeply satisfying.

Still, it strikes me that while the events I imagined
in my childhood and youth
have largely come to pass, they've done so much
less loudly
and with considerably less grandeur in fruition
than I'd envisioned when I began.
And I sometimes wonder: Is this all that was ever
in my plan?

An old man now, closing the circle, and the world
has not changed in the directions I thought I'd been
empowered to move it—
not by so much as the span of my hand.

11-5-13

With All His Joys and Hopes

"Who is that friendly old guy in the picture?"
For a split second I actually thought that.
"With my wife and daughter?"
Then I thought, "He looks really friendly! Oh!"
The hint of a shock. "It's me." Wow! Mild
cognitive impairment or at least
a slip of dissonance.
I mean, I see myself every day in the mirror.
For yours I've watched my beard turn
white, my hair go grey.
But to see me this way side-by-side with my wife
and daughter in a snapshot! Something got
out of phase about the way
I've been framing my self-image. I imagine that's
to be laid at the feet of spirit, which, while
maturing, nonetheless in
some sense never ages.
Right there's the increasing decoupling of the
actual and imagined, outer and inner,
graphically displayed,
instantiated between the photo and my gaze.
Is that friendly old man the same person
this earlier picture shows
of the five-year-old in cowboy costume on the
pony,
that old black-and-white on my daughter's

bedroom wall? Yes. The very same,
with all his joys and hopes.

1-20-14

The "I" Is the Only Presence

Why do memories fade as the past slips back?
Because the "I" is always present.
Why is the future vague?
Because the "I" is the only Presence.[110]

I pass through it, or it transverses me.
I say "I" and "me," though these are the "I's"
conceptions
of itself as temporal, which it is pleased to be,
so long as it may also keep its ripened,
timeless essence.

11-19-14

---

[110] This reference is to a fascinating analysis of Presence as the Present in the contemporary philosopher Stanley Rosen's "Metaphysics in Ordinary Language."

Nostalgia

At some time after its passing, what was rich or
good about the past becomes extruded,
drawn out from that fraught or even tragic context
within which such sweetness first obtruded,
it may be, largely unremarked amid those clouds of
occurrences in which it came to birth and
was occluded,
and may only become more adequately known as
that is observed to rarify and rise, recruited
from the mass of static through which, initially, it
moved, and in retrospect might be more clearly
viewed
as hierophantic, drifting upward or hovering like a
golden haze or halo casting light about a darkened
room.
Then all that's passed, all anguish and confusion, is
seen to have been necessary exactly as it stood,
all that happened worthwhile, not in and of itself,
we might conclude,
but for what it birthed, matured, and bloomed.

It's not that in nostalgia we are deluded. It's that
Goodness, both generating and using such a
softening mood,

shows us something of the reason for a world at all — vertical translocation and a benevolence of transmuting.

12-17-10

Achilles for Priam

In moments of accumulated and over-topping
clarity, I fall
in-love with all I've known and all I know to be.
Enemies vanish, even disease.
In place of threat, what I see is a vast, anguished
community, terrified mutuality,
competition for, for this world at least, an illusion
of well-being,
or being of any degree. What I feel is comradely
love, like Achilles for Priam[111] that night on the
beach,
a surge of empathy, compelling to me as that
mighty slosh and heave
which rises upward in answer to the moon's
allure, as she dazzles and glides
above the sea.
I see what I think Homer perceived: when Troy
burned, inexorably,
the Achaeans also drank deeply of grief.

Beneath this film of matter, out of which each is
manufactured and becomes discreet,
we are one solitary thing — this, of a species we
cannot name, of which we

---

[111] Priam: The king of Troy during the Trojan War. Homer's
"Iliad" depicts Priam coming to the tent of Achilles in the
middle of the night to beg from him the body of Hector,
Priam's son, whom Achilles had slain.

cannot authentically speak.
Beyond our antagonisms, human being and beast,
I sense a dimension just out of reach,
a reality spoken of for the most part in whispers,
across an indistinct boundary between
what has been, is, or ever will be,
and what may never be entered except in death,
or perhaps in depths of dreamless sleep.
There, Hector and Achilles, Agamemnon and
Priam, Jews, Christians, and jihadis — all this
dynamic and dangerous feast —
dissipate in darkness, begin again in light. There,
where they were, perfect amity is —
everlasting and unbroken peace.

3-18-12

Goodnight

Goodnight.
See you in the morning,
after the night I dread,
after the suffocating blackness,
after the life in me has ebbed
like a ring of smoke or mist,
or been withdrawn
below, beneath,
and utterly extinguished,
out of mind and nullified,
erased to zero…

and then dawned once more
with singing birds, such great Light,
and that indescribable sky!
I step out upon fresh lawn
as if from some frigid cavity
filled with ghosts.
That now seems fantastic, almost
forgotten.
Now I do forget.

Goodnight. Goodnight.
See you in the Morning!

3-18-10

Hindsight

I. The Purpose of Our Pasts

It is often only in hindsight, from a hilltop looking
back,
that we are finally able to discern the significance
of a series of events or actions.
At the time, we were mostly floundering forward —
this, from this to that,
not without perhaps some planning,
yet nonetheless in hazard
with circumstances we were handed.
Add to that distractions,
multiple causative factors —
as well, that which we call randomness or chance.
It is not possible to empirically announce that
the pattern
equals meaning which we descry, we have just
now imposed
upon that riotous discordance,
or if it was destined all along, and we, at or past
some grand
crescendoing, are enabled to see the truth of it from
our presently higher vantage.
I suspect the latter — that deeper goals are the
reason for time's passing,
and that our mishandling or semi-conscious
blundering was guided by an
import-driven tack.

Hindsight, in actuality, is our experience of
foresight on the part of That
Which fashions us, gazing back upon our
futures, the purpose of our pasts.

II. What We Meant

Not that we will ever know the full extent of what
we meant,
or what was meant for us to speak and be.
Meaning comes in manifold layers, only some of
which may
reach our consciousness, like zones and mansions
of the sea.
At times, it seems, these slip cross-currented with
other goals
and dreams, intermixed perhaps with feelings not
our own, and visions of Elysium —
in any case, pleromatic functionally, too vast for us
increasingly,
and shading off at last toward some fantastic,
living Mystery.

11-19-12

Love and Death

It is true that Beauty and Truth — as well, those
many
fields which spread out in multitudes before us —
by converging and diverging paths eventually
bring
us to an end in wordless awe or wonder.
It is truer still that Love, after certain crucibles of
fire,
sterilities, falsehoods, or perhaps straightforwardly,
deposits us in states of self-surpassing —
that is to say, fulfillment of what we all once were,
and
strove to be again, which is, as Love unfolds by
stages
or all at once, reduced to intermittent flashes,
and we are free from ourselves, our passions, our
fears
and hopes, ambitions, acquisitions, exultations,
envies, satieties, and triumphs.

Yes, Love is Death. Death is Love.
In Death we are loved,
and we will know it.

12-5-09

A Dark Road

When you come to a dark road rife with danger,
you have two provisionally sane possibilities.
One is to switch on a flashlight or kindle a torch
if you have one of these, and push on through.
You might just make it.
The other is to turn around and come back out of
there, perhaps a bit shaken, but still more or less
in one piece.
Whatever you choose, you're not going to be able
to fake it.

3-10-15

The Worth of Each Human Life

The worth of each human life falls away in
reverberation until it becomes
magnified
magnified
magnified beyond exceeding.
It is like surf generated on the far side of a
limitless sea, breaking colossally
against recalcitrant and stony finitude, yet
not like surf because its energy is never
dissipated, but grows in force
to climax,
or always was incalculably tremendous, and
perhaps because of that could not
be estimated in the fullness
of its amplitude.
Unlike waves of any species which scatter and
trail off to entropy
in the void, the worth of each human being
echoes in eternity,
such that no human life is lost, but all transcribed
and raised from lower latitudes
to higher measures of geography, indeed to
absoluteness,
and brought before that infinite Cartographer
Who termlessly esteems it.

2-6-11

The Gaze

Unblinking, It fixed Its gaze upon him, looked
at him concertedly without wavering,
albeit through a continuous digitalish shimmering,
across the surface of the orbit's glazing,
the way a gust of breeze skitters above a shivering
lake,
or that nervous quake beneath the hide of horses
when they're curbed and stayed.
It put his hopes for safety in definitive abeyance,
and acquainted
him most intimately with his self-engendered fate.

5-22-15

You Needn't Be Afraid

You needn't be afraid of the far side of
death's door.
Although you don't remember it well,
you've been there before.
Where you are going is where you already
are, before, during, and after
your dropping down here, where you've
had an adventure and become
pretty thoroughly distracted
by the to-ing and fro-ing, the hubbub, the
dashes of light and shadow.
You needn't be afraid of growing more
quiet. Climb the stairs.
When the door opens, walk through it.
Deep breath,
one more step. See? You're Home!

9-14-14

George Wilkerson's Passing

Old George Wilkerson, the Classical scholar, renowned,
though not uncriticized, for his interpretations
of Homer, counted out by the Academy for his commentary
on Callimachus,[112] nonetheless had been justly
credited with prodigious erudition.

Now, like all mortals, he was facing his end. His wife
was asleep in the chair by his bed. His three
children would be arriving as soon as they could, afraid
that by the time they reached the hospital he
would already be dead.

He was, as they say, in and out of it, heavily drugged to
at least put a dent in his pain. He was dying of
cancer. It could have been any kind for all it
mattered to him.
As it turned out, it was cancer of the brain.

He became conscious of a shaking in his room. His first
thought was "earthquake," his second, that it was

---

[112] Callimachus (310-240 B.C.E.): The much noted Hellenistic
poet, critic, and scholar at the Library of Alexandria

him. It was actually neither, although he was certainly
involved. His body was not trembling — rather, something
more consequential than flesh, bone, or skin.

Suddenly, through the gleaming linoleum of the floor
of his room, through a cleft at the foot of the bed
where he lay, which he couldn't see for the footboard,
rattling various instruments, steel and plastic contraptions,
dripping bottles and bags, autoclaved trays, rose
a black hulk like a submarine making an emergency
blow, then crashing back on the turbulent waves. That shot
upward, blew to confetti the sound-proofing tiles
of the ceiling, and wrought twisted wreckage of their aluminum
frames, a column of night so dark no light escaped
or reflected
from it, then settled, yet still towered, winking and
quavering, unfolded, focused, and took on shapes George
could more or less recognize through his drug-induced daze,
albeit these were unnervingly strange — indeed,
shapes not seen in this world for nearly two

thousand years:
four black horses, black chariot, and Hades,
a figure of doom,
standing upright in his terrible car, gripping the
reins with iron fingers. Black was his breastplate,
his cape,
grieves and his face, black was his beard, his
helmet and plumes.

Darkness reeked from the awful scene in concentric
halos,
bands of midnight, emanations, fumes of mist-
shrouded hedges, toadstools, rain-pregnant sod,
earthworms,
grubs, skunks, wolf packs, wet stones and sticks.

He was not alone. In the chariot, which lurched
forward
and back as the horses stamped and shivered their
shins, and jangled their bridles and champed their
bits, the form of
Persephone loomed, bride of death, yet nonetheless
the bringer of spring.
She was bathed in light, which seemed to arise
from within. The glowing robe she wore over her
hair,
illumined by flowers, with vines arrayed, shone
with the sun
she had borne underground the day she was
kidnapped and raped by her lord.

It was she who spoke to old George, out-fitted in his hoses
and clamps. She said in a voice as warm as July
afternoons, "Do not be afraid of my husband's demeanor,
nor his decision to make an appearance to you. Instead,
George, rejoice! Yes, he means the end of your
earthly existence which, in any case, you knew
would be coming soon.
I appear with him, and conduct all souls who have
been reasonably good,
once he's delivered the decisive blow, to an
enchanted wood where spring and summer are
always in bloom.
Life is at ease as long as you wish it. Then, if you
desire a change,
you may move on to autumn or winter, take up
new challenges, brave new dangers. If you're
homesick
for Earth, you may reincarnate. Fulfill all your
dreams,
grow the spirit, become an arhat or saint, gradually
thinning, and fade into that vastness of Light and
Bliss beyond
these dimensions of ghosts, bogies, and shades.
Finally,
tired from the burden of singular identity, however
amplified and rendered more generous, you may

wish to
be nothing and become one with the Source.
Though
I have not taken that road myself, I am assured it is
anything but onerous."

George lifted his head as well as he was able and
rasped, "Persephone,
guide me to Elysium. Hades, strike now.
Make my body a corpse.
Send my best self to God!"

When his wife awoke, George had already expired.
The room
was as she'd come to expect it, but also
extraordinarily quiet.

1-12-14

Her Vanishing

By subtle means, of which the she she knew as she
was largely ignorant,
scarcely heralded from her perspective, her
attention shifted like a breeze-borne leaf,
equally, as if insurgency from the molten mantel
underneath
had risen without warning, though intimations had
been delivered with some regularity.
She stood obliquely, stunned, without a word or
whisper, beheld an ancient door,
the like of which heretofore had only shimmered
through her inner eye in deepest sleep,
a self-disclosure and her witnessing of this.
Wither-shins she bent the glimmer of her eye to
face the portal,
opening space beyond unknown to her, dimensions
of reality within its compass
which she had never dared to think of, far less
picture to herself.
Amazed, she edged forward,
drifted not straight nor parallel to lines with which
she was familiar,
but took a turn, vectored left around the corner of a
star-strewn wall or curtain
defying structure and linearity, then pushed the
door ajar with neither

sorrow nor regret, entered, and ceased to be entirely.

1-7-05

Apocalypse

When lions lie down with lambs, lions will no
longer be lions; neither will lambs be lambs.
When protons and electrons nestle together, the
character of each will be banished.
When Neanderthals and mammoths reach
reconciliation, tusks and spears will be shattered.
When oppressors and oppressed share the same
table, both will be transfigured.
When spirit and matter cease making a clatter,
what was known as reality will vanish.

12-6-11

Without Fear

We come through Nature from who knows where,
are formed by what we bring and what we
encounter here.
We pass beyond this into some other medium, a
mixture of what we were in origin and what
we became with the years.
Jesus said, "Be in the world, but not of it." He said,
"Be wayfarers without fear."[113]

4-21-11

---

[113] This is a reference to a supposed saying of Jesus in the
Gnostic Gospel of Thomas, chapter 42.

Metamorphoses

By Death

By death we are humiliated.
By death we are exalted.[114]

2-21-14

---

[114] This is an adaptation of an ancient Egyptian proverb.

Who Is That "I"?

Who is that "I" that watches me, and
by that watching makes me?

The same, Who when my life is done,
will shake and then awake me.

3-23-16

Amazed

She'd lived a full life, and was on the verge
of world-weariness and boredom.
It struck her then like a hammer blow, although
it was soft as silk in its self-disclosure.
She sat amazed until the thought had formed.
She let it in. It was like an echo
both far away and immediately beside her. It
wafted through her like a breath of spring,
but clear, definitive, sober.
"There's more," it said.
It was spoken only once. But this was enough
to begin her renovation.

1-12-16

Teotihuacanos

And when those ancient Teotihuacanos,[115] who
lived their lives as nightmares or as dreams,
fell into their soft, soft beds, slipped off, discarded
flesh and skin, and knew the gift of
endless, unearthly sleep,
they were reborn as fragile butterflies with multi-
colored paper wings. For these
Totality became the sun and the all-enfolding
medium of a spirit-congested breeze.

3-23-16

---

[115] Teotihuacanos: The inhabitants of the pre-Maya city in
central Mexico

On Filling the Hollow That Was Once the Mediterranean

What can I say to you in the throes of your grief?
Be empty as an oceanless sea.[116]
Don't expect to be filled, or even hope for that.
Sit on the stones, disconsolate, flattened.
Feel vast emptiness. Do not wish.
Appreciate but do not succumb to its desolation.
Touch detachment with your fingertips,
but do not embrace it, as if lack were a healer.
It isn't.
Accept it as what it is not — lush, alive, teeming.
At the moment, you are none of these.
Slowly, imperceptibly in the beginning, some refreshing
fluid will seep up from beneath,
or trickle down over the blasted rim. If you're okay
with that, it will gradually fill.
It will not be the sea with which you were
innocently intimate.
But it will be the sea that you need.

8-21-15

---

[116] Geologists believe that there was a time in the distant past when the basin which now holds the Mediterranean Sea was dry.

Cadmus' Transfiguration

Ovid[117] says that Cadmus,[118] the founder of Thebes,
after years of hard self-exile,
was turned into a snake by the gods because he'd
finally allowed himself to become mindful of
the possibility that the serpent he'd slain in order
to establish and populate his city
had been a Divine hierophany, the animal disguise
of some ancient deity.

It's true that he'd made that admission to his wife
as a kind of simultaneous affirmation-and-denial.
"If the snake I slaughtered was a god, then I'll be
a serpent too!" he'd said with perhaps a little too
much bile.

Whatever exactly and why that happened, if
Cadmus turned a god into humanity, God changed
him into an animal.
You might think that was bad for Cadmus until
you realize that the Greeks believed all serpents are
immortal.

---

[117] Ovid (43 B.C.E.-18 C.E.): A famous Roman poet, and author
of "Metamorphoses"
[118] Cadmus: The legendary founder of the ancient Greek city
of Thebes, who populated his new city by sowing the teeth of
the Castalian Serpent which he had slain. The teeth sprouted,
and grew up from the ground as warriors.

I might go further and suggest that God is actually
willing to be sacrificed to become all and every
member of our species,
and, while we may shrink from returning the favor,
God anyway gifts us with divinity.

4-24-14

Epitaph Inscribed on a Cinerarium

To paraphrase Ausonius, the Roman poet:[119]

"Here lie I. Well, not entirely. Instead, a
significantly altered rendition—something grey
and flakey.
For now at least I have some affinity with this,
albeit not exclusively.
In any case, I ask you to pour a libation of wine and
spikenard on this testament to
our mutual mortality
as the flesh—that is to say, as bone-and-meat—
and, as well, to hie hitherward balsam and
red roses.
In my Essence, I luxuriate in unending spring. I
have not died, you see.
What I have actually done is rather drastically
changed my location."

12-20-15

---

[119] The text is here adapted from a quotation of one of the
Roman poet Ausonius' tomb inscriptions in J.M.C. Toynbee's
"Death and Burial in the Roman World." Ausonius' dates are
c.310-c.395 C.E.

Bell-Krater: The Resurrection
of Persephone
(Attic, Red-figure, c. 440 B.C.E.)

With eerie grace, wraith-like, stately, Persephone
rises
at night's nadir from the Underworld, the
geography
and contents of which are forbidden and
unspeakable.

Her spinal column is ram-rod erect, as if supported
artificially,
her left knee flexed to place the foot's next
tread upon
the black-swathed surface of the Earth.

She regally ascends, yet somehow unnaturally,
statue-like,
as if immobilized by what she's seen
and done Below,
mummyish, robotically, from a cleft
unbreachable —

as well, incapable of discovery by those, both
divine and mortal,
who have not yet experienced, or wished for, that
harrowing of shades
and shadows which emerges as the underside of
Psyche,

wherein the person ceases.
She lets fall a subdued brilliance from within,
as do those
three above who await her reappearance, orangish-
red,

color of the fired clay, sub-ignited figures, flame-
like yet
restrained, carefully delineated by the painter
against
that smothering nothingness that goes on and on
forever,

and stops only at their edges, where being is
starkly declared
within the stillness of that midnight medium
of the not yet thought,
imagined, or perhaps never will be said.

Hermes[120] stands above/behind the rising Kore,
kerykeion[121]
pointing toward the ground, signifying that his
mission of retrieval
has been accomplished, that Persephone is free of
death as final,
and resurrected.

---

[120] Hermes: The ancient Greek god of wayfaring souls, who
led the deceased down into the Underworld. In this case, he
has guided Persephone through her resurrection back onto
the earth plane.
[121] Kerykeion: Hermes' magic wand

He looks not at her, nor along the sideways-facing line of his painted
fellow-figures, but out from the two dimensions of the krater's surface,
straight at us, helmet wings
flight-spread,
fixing us with his hypnotic gaze, undoubtedly conveying a message — what?

I think, that Spring has come for all of us, although we will taste death. Like Persephone, we shall be wished back among the living by loved-ones' yearnings — these, and the boundless Benevolence of Zeus.

Willowy Hecate,[122] holding aloft two torches against the
stifling darkness, beholding the re-arisen heiress full-in-the-face,
backs toward the maiden's mother, Demeter, leading
Persephone toward the magnet of that Soul that refused her daughter's death,
and to a tearful re-uniting.

---

[122] Hecate: The ancient Greek goddess of witchcraft and crossroads

So may all who undergo these Mysteries know
God's infinite Love and
unrestricted Giving.

7-5-14

The King of Crows

I have witnessed crows like a plague of death-
betokening
miniature dinosaurs throng down upon a beech to
keen
for their un-treed king —

unsalvageably erased from the realm of the bright-
bristling
sun,

collapsed in a heap of ink-jet plumage, post-
biologic, stiff as
stone, no longer sentient, smoking, plutonic,
reeking,

feathers dimly glistening in a merciless light,
exceedingly
well-dusted.

I have clapped palms to organs of audition in order
to shutter
their netherworldly screeching, their unbridled
seething

at that earthward leap each is obliged to make,
their unrestrainable grieving,

mustered and billowing before that fate which
looms without
warning, splits atoms and brains, that gash in

tumultuous
being

that suddenly gapes the circumferenceless circle,
unheeding
of pleas by man or beast.

That breast-bolting rage is the wailing of all things.
Nothing
evades it, not even those tipplers of nectar and
ambrosia
on high ivory seats

seven stories aloft over math, physics, and biology,
feigning
indifference to time and space —

not you or I, our tribes, parents, daughters and
sons, whole
galaxies, not dogs dying in the streets, not viruses,
protons,
nor our gravest achievements.

All are extinguished — the cruel, the kind, the rich,
the humble,
even the wisest.

Don't think what has been done to us does not go
all the way
up to the God of Love. Lamenting is His for the

intractable
monstrosity of what was bequeathed

us by our clamoring for existence in a universe
made manifest
of midnight and blaze.

He awakens the life-lost, re-cloaks the king of the
crows, restores
and unbetrays him
in magnificent and transfigured state.

9-30-15

The Only Cure There Is

I lie here in my last bed, strengthless,
panting for all I loved on earth
with unmitigatable sorrow at its elapsing —
not mine. It was unsurpassable,
truly, all that I have traversed of it — its
joys, its grievances, the pageantry
I have breathed, touched, lived — Nature,
and all the souls I have been privileged
to accompany, and who have accompanied
me, on our journeys, singular as diverse!
It was a miracle, the whole of it, and I will
not know it, or anything like it, again.
You think I'm panting because I'm dying.
It's true I cannot catch my breath.
But, underneath, that's not because my
respiration's failing. It's because I was
so in-love, and I know — oh how I know! —
this I'm undergoing is the only cure there is.

4-26-15

Rather More than Less Felicitous

By many accounts, we do not die alone.
Loved ones are said to arrive in order to reclaim us.
Our moments of mortality may in fact be
crammed with entities who've preceded us
in that grand disenfranchisement of the body and
subsequent transfer of our terrestrial information
to another mode of being.
Many if not most of these may not be wholly
human.
At least they are anonymous.

Jacob saw a staircase alive with demigods,[123]
winking on
and off, flood-lights shining stridently at the
bottom,
over-bright and manifestly dangerous.
I do not know who or what comes through that
door
the dying often see up
near the ceiling in a corner of the room. I hope
whatever

---

[123] This is a rather loose extension of the legendary night encounter of the Hebrew patriarch Jacob with divine beings. The passage can be found in the Hebrew Testament, the book of Genesis, chapter 28, verses 10-17.

decloaks and fills the scene of my terminal
arrangements
will be rather more than less felicitous.

10-12-15

Fantastically Re-speeched

I will be silent in my demise, and cease
what presently speaks as me.
But on death's other side, I will be re-spoken
and fantastically re-speeched.

9-11-13

Threshold

I

Step up to that transubstantiating Threshold
which intervenes between the you you
dream and another
You writ larger.
Tread upon that ancient metamorphosing stone,
and be drawn beyond it. Even if it's
dark out there,
and there is shivering, tears, or at least some
misgivings, on the other side is exaltation
of the soul!

II

Or when you step upon that golden Touchstone
which
translates every now into some light-washed
Ever-after,
and your soul exults and soars

into a sun-combusting mist just beyond the door,
and
opens to a dawn upon storm-tossed
morning gardens,
you will cry aloud, chant and sing, or roar!

III

Could I but touch that Stone with the tip of my toe,
and that way thrust up without heartache,
suffering, or regress,

and sing without first weeping,

I would be willing to change this very instant. I
would be willing to make alterations to my
comportment.
I would be willing to repent,

and gladly love with my whole being!

11-6-14

She Died

They said she was dead, but it was they who'd died
relative to her location.
For her, death was a deliverance — in fact, a birth
forward
and backwards — which is to say,
back to being herself, yet, while indisputably also
someone
significantly more commodious,
more knowledgeable, immeasurably happier, and
posted
to a higher station.
She departed alright. The eyes dimmed, the face
fell. Yet
the brilliance of her course
electrified the sky. It seems to me unquestionable
she was
granted immortality —
and that, without delay.

1-6-05

Your Fame (for My Mother)

You gained some small honors in your life in Rock
Island,
and local fame among generations
of your students, those who prized and loved you,
especially
those whom you initiated into the mysterious inner
sanctum
of high literature, its analysis and production, how
words can be
lathed, planed, and shaped to re-present the hidden
movements
of the soul, as it shifts behind the scenes through its
earthen forms
toward spiritual rewards — how it stops along the
way to furtively observe,
stammers shy messages, or blurts or bleats these to
those it takes for
soul-mates, even to complete strangers — and all the
twists and machinations of its
characters on the page.
I say, how you were loved, albeit parochially,
and by these two sons you
raised,
by your parents, sister, nephews,
nieces,
and your friends — how then you gradually slipped
toward terminal invisibility,

and finally disappeared behind the veil. Your
honors were
anonymous by the standards of the larger world,
radically unnoticed
on that even vaster scale of history, to say nothing
of the cosmos —
infinitesimal, it is true, and yet your focus
was the human
heart and mind, of which there is nothing greater.
You gave
the best you were, and that was more valuable to
your Creator
than all that calliope of galaxies, the famous figures
of human history,
democrats and tyrants. You were the best there is,
has been,
or will be. The universe was made for you. Your
fame
is absolute where you now dwell, within those
swells
illuminate of that oceanic and fathomless Divinity!

3-3-15

Wondrous an Occasion

When I stand dissolved and recommenced before
the Seat of Deity,
how will my deeds be evaluated?
I mean deeds of culture, of intellect, of morality and
ethics, of charity,
of physics and the psyche?
I have healed and I have damaged; I have been
faithful and I have betrayed;
I have sown darkness and I have kindled
light.
My sense of self has been inextricably inter-tied
with people
and the innumerable things of this
raucous reality
in which light and shadow transposition rather
facilely —
sorrowfulness, anxiety, triumph, gaiety, sickness,
health, hunger and satiety.
I say inextricably, and yet I've also known at least
partial and
momentary translocation, or at any rate a level
higher.

Has it been enough, my life I mean, to merit
reconstruction,
re-formation into greater amplitude of being and
society?
Have I done well enough to earn a mostly

favorable decision
when my life is weighed in the pan, all my days
and nights,
against Divine ideals for me? Will God forgive me?
Will I get
a passing grade—not a ticket to Paradise perhaps,
but a
place to catch my breath, then initiate
a process of rehabilitation, an enhanced program of
anamnesis,
it may be, by which I might be enabled to remember and even celebrate?
If I am judged acceptable to receive this state of
consciousness
and well-being, to live into whatsoever fresh bones
and blood I may be changed,
I will certainly embrace with gratitude my new
identity, and,
traversing hoped-for fields of light by means of
tornadic wings displayed
and psychic operations, I shall reach Home at last,
sun-saturate,
diaphanous indeed upon so wondrous an occasion!

4-25-10

All Along Intended

Have you committed very grave sins — inured
to the suffering of your fellow human beings,
cruelty toward them even, torture, murder?

God knows why you became to misshapen, and
the what and who that made of you a monster.
But, so I'm commanded, I cannot deny you
Heaven.

Did you rape — women, men? Did you grind people
under for the sake of your wallet, or for power or
status?

God knows why you came to that distortion of
your natal innocence. Nevertheless, I am not
authorized to deny you renewal and
transcendence.

Were you dishonest in your business dealings?
Were you a highwayman or a thief? Were you
brutal to your spouse or children?

God knows how you arrived at such un-grieved
grief. Still, I am unqualified to condemn your
unbelief.

Did you inflict pain and unnecessary death on
those creatures less sentient than yourself?
Did you tear the wings from flies? Did you
burn bats

alive, poison cats, or laugh at cattle in the
slaughter house?

God knows how you came to feel so superior, how
your heart was changed to ice. All the same, it's
rumored you will enter Paradise.

Did you refuse to accept responsibility for your
deeds? Do you still believe "Do unto others
before they do unto to you"? Are you yet,
even on your deathbed,
a narcissistic horse's ass?

God knows why you became such detritus and
trash.
Yet, there is no one of sufficient moral magnitude
to deny your skyward passage.

Were you unable to rise above your animal
instincts, tame the reptile at the base of
your brain? Were you incapacitated
by the wounded child within?
Were you unable to become fully human?

God knows why you became so thoroughly a
villain. C.S. Lewis[124] said that Hell is a

---

[124] C.S. Lewis (1898-1963): The famous and highly influential
British Christian theologian, apologist, writer, and
Chairperson of Medieval and Renaissance Literature at
Cambridge

human being dying of thirst in a
rainstorm.

I am not empowered to deny you refreshment. You
have denied it to yourself.

Still, with al-Ghazali and many of the more
merciful and most humane, I will affirm the
possibility of your rehabilitation.

If you have harmed someone I have loved, I do not
believe I could forgive you. But I do believe
there is a God, far darker than you,
Who is waiting in the shadows of
your imprisoned mind to do it.

He is infinitely more cruel than you, infinitely more
severe, yet also infinitely prepared to take you in,
and, on condition of your gaining sufficient
insight and wisdom, make of you the
triumph He'd all along intended.

11-3-13

The Judgment

When I am presented to myself as a whole and in
finely
granulated detail, all the things I knew by reason,
senses,
and imagination —
by these same agencies, the things I knew that
never reached
the short-hand maneuvering of my intentions —
as well,
those things I never knew at any level, which
nonetheless
pertained to me, without pretension in my
profounder identity,
which perhaps I should have known but for my
finitude,
yet may become reacquainted with now that I've
been forced to
change my attitude,
I shall be stunned
to speechless awe, overwhelmed by that Totality,
darkness and light.
And then I'll pass, thankfully I should think, from
what is left of me
to That Which is Entire.

10-29-13

Boundlessly Fulfilled in the Life You Lived

I would say to the dying, you are loved,
and will be illimitably missed,
but you have more important things to
do right now than consoling us —
that this
must be your only focus: going out into
that greater Light-and-Brightness,
transitioning from the animal to some larger
mode of embarkation, which surpasses
human limits.
Whatever clime you reach, whatever form
is given, whatever sins remembered
and instantaneously or in the course of
time forgiven,
you shall become a holy, august creature,
immensely satisfied, and boundlessly
fulfilled in the life you lived.

12-21-14

Mani and Me

Mani[125] had a celestial Twin — numinous, lunar,
divinely wise,
his comforter, counselor, himself before his earthly
re-presentation from that strangely beautiful state
in which we are all ourselves and yet each other,
and then became encapsulate within this
coagulate phase of energy
we call matter.

Mani's Twin was always watching him, and, when
he died,
would assure his escape from the corpse, re-absorb
him, and cause him, transmogrified as Him, to
live for all eternity in Heaven.

Mani was judged to be what we would now term
schizophrenic.
I view him as inspired.

Indeed, I have myself experienced something like a
light-exuding
Double, dwelling in some starry realm above my
day-to-day,
comforting, counseling, inspiring, watching, and
correcting me — some hyper-Me from Whom

---

[125] Mani (c.216-274 C.E.): Mani was the founder of
Manichaeism, an ancient religion which combined features of
Zoroastrianism and Christianity, and which continued to
survive in Central Asia into the Middle Ages.

I have descended, and to Whom I will go
when my world-traversing is completed.

What's more, I know to some degree alternative
selves, related
to my present identity, likewise descended from
that timeless Me, who have been, are now, or will
be taken up when the flesh springs free of me,
and these bones which held my earthly
form together fail.

All of these impress themselves upon me as
conditions warrant.

That celestial Me Who is more than me, I do my
best to serve,
and trust, in moments of greatest clarity, to retrieve
me when my embodied tasks expire.

I too then might be mad like Mani.

I prefer to see such envisionings as instants of
expansiveness and rapture.

8-11-12

Haven't You Seen Yet?

Haven't you seen yet how when you die you
become
this magnified post-mortem presence,
fiery, gold, five miles high,
with rushing flame-enveloped plumage—mauve,
chartreuse,
indigo, neon-green, a spray of pinions
light-years wide,
oiled and jewelried hair flying in a wild cascade
over folds
and filigreed borders of a skyey robe
embroidered with signs
for life-forces, images of living things, animated as
it flows—
all that which you have known or will,
soaring unbridled
in an infinite void, a lunging throat of glimmering
scales,
flashing births of galaxies from ecstatic
eyes,
everything seen deeply, radiating atmospheres,
torrential
blazings casting forth, although arrested,
wise and kind,
your skin as smooth as polished glass, reflecting all
that is,
will be, all that has passed, and continuously

rising,
rising forever toward Limitlessness and that
Promise,
inexhaustible and immediate, of consummating
Light?

2-9-12

Lions and Lambs

Lions and lambs recline, side-by-side or
intertwined, essence with essence,
winged perhaps, as solid as they might seem,
or like comingled mists,

grey, fresh as dew, rainbow-haloed, shoulder-to-
shoulder, arm-in-arm upon respective *klinas*,[126]
and share whatever sustenance they may wish.

Pensive occasionally, yet often they may laugh and
speak of secrets, species-based,
in grunts, bleats, roars full-throated, or in sounding
words or even whispers.

They carry within these transfigured forms the
heritage of their biologies,
when they first emerged upon the Earth, one in
terror of starvation,
the other of that first one's fatal kiss.

Yet here, countenance-to-countenance, wide-
browed, bi-pedal, with grasping hands,
backs like dolphins,' smooth as silk, elongated like
eels', they slip

---

[126] Klinas: Ancient Greek, subsequently Roman, dining
couches on which guests reclined while eating

confidently beyond their pasts, honoring what each
to the other once had meant,
wiser than those necessities of their enfleshments,

more generous than their genes had permitted
in that world of their birthing
as Nature, its pangs and needs. No longer bound
by that regime, they now discover friendship,
even love, as siblings

of a larger family. And when their conversation's
finished, they lift up on something
like a wavering of wings, and sing together in that
ebony and hierophantic shimmering

above, leonine, ungulate, or man-like heads, rush
up into that auroral sheening which
has no limit, in each other's arms, flippers,
flagellum, appendages whatsoever,
know embrace of Love,

and endlessness of Bliss.

1-25-11

This Flesh

This flesh, this fold of skin, this dimple, that mole I
knew as you,
no other — and your soul, precious beyond
expression or construing,
strong and fragile —
the former now unresponsive, that second
absconded, leaving
only this foreignness, wreckage, together cast aside
like abandoned
dolls or a scattering of *ushabti*[127] —
this cool mask, grey as dust or clay, careless now,
as if nothing
which transpired in that unity of blood and soul
which you had
been had ever mattered.
Unreflecting now, your eyes which once spoke,
illustrative of your
presence there behind the frontal lobes, your laugh
lines and your
smiling lips, inanimate, which before this debacle
of your nulling
mirrored up and outward
what you loved and hated, wished for, and
engaged us both and

---

[127] Ushabti: Ancient Egyptian statuettes or doll-like
representations of human figures buried with the deceased,
and believed to become magically activated in the Afterlife in
order to fulfill the deceased's manual duties there

others in that vivid dance that was your living self,
that person
beloved, one center merely of everything that is, I
recognize —
still, the only reality significant to me —
these are sealed irrevocably and decommissioned,
and will not,
in all the future of this useless universe, be re-
imagined. What
fantastic interface existed
then between flesh and spirit that has been cast
past reclamation, that
earth I touched, smelled, heard, tasted, the
presence wholly there —
the meat
and blood and hair you were! How am I to descry
some other "I"
of you that might have survived the hearsay of
these rigid fingers,
stone-cold palms that once
caressed my face anterior to this bereavement? Am
I to imagine you
continue with some version of that triune brain by
which our intimacies
were inspired,
by which you were so richly modulated, textured,
toned, conveyed
in your ferocities, hungers, plenitudes, qualms, and
graces? How much

less was understood — and that, idiosyncratically —
of who you really were when
you were giving birth, working in the kitchen,
running the business,
holding me or kissing me goodnight!
How I shudder at the thought of you transfigured,
amplified, reallocated
to some higher plane, equipped with outlandish
organs other than these
deactivated features
by which I loved you! If you survive away from me
in such or other
unconventional spaces, in form and makeup
altered beyond my
recognition or my capacity
to renew our former intimacy, I shall wonder what
strange chicanery has
been deployed, and to what end precisely, that that
every-day you with
whom I felt familiar,
at times at least, with whom I intermingled on the
sofa, whom I adored,
without the slightest inkling of this waiting
strangeness, the hour of its
arrival, or its rapacity,
should prove expugnable, as I myself shall also
surely be. These stairs we
climbed to bed each night. I stand at the bottom,
eyes narrowed at that

unstirring void above
which should be occupied by you. But you have
climbed up higher, beyond
the landing and the ceiling, beyond light and
shadow, mass-less now,
unsusceptible.
I am bereft of you, but do not wish to see your
dazzlement. Blinded by my
tears and by my fear of what might constitute your
transformation, I
just want our love
again as it was when we both were human.
Without you I am immeasurably
diminished. I must go on changing alone, while
you are past that now
and indestructible.

3-8-03

Transcendent Validation

Whether the soul or spirit is naturally immortal or
is snuffed out
with the asphyxiation of the brain,
and then reconstituted on the basis of data, stored
and retrieved,
in that spectacular remake termed resurrection,
the process of either seems significantly fraught to
me — on the one
hand, de-coupling from a functional infinity of
neurons,
overcoming the swoon said to be caused by this,
then, bodiless,
at least initially, gradually regaining one's
orientation —
or going under entirely unto nothingness, stripped
down below the
molecular level to absolute zero,
then someone tapping your shoulder even as
they're reassembling it —
light, your first inhalation! I can't imagine how
either one might be accomplished.
At the same time, it seems preposterous to me that
some particularly dramatic
series of events would not be employed to grant
the human being
wished-for climax and transcendent validation.

1-29-12

Luminosity

Interrupted by death, transubstantiation, or that,
we say,
which takes its natural course; either way, we none
of us gains completion.
But there, aloft, we image all potentials, those at
least we
know as bright and good, which would have made
us demigods or angels here in season.
In that alternative dimension these are neither
possible,
impossible, nor probable, but real, and this
truncated
life per se, devoid of rhyme or reason,
fulfillment finds upon such future luminosity as
that Good Deity
which emitted us to begin with shall arrange
henceforth—
this, by cudgel, severity of discussion, or by most
intimate persuasion.

7-22-09

The Cause of Death

There is only one cause of death, and that is Deity.
God uses whatever tools
might be at hand to ensconce us, whelm us, catch
us up, and remove
us from our present medium. And here are we
imagining
that our current moorings
represent normality, as if high, wild, and gusty
vastness
were alien to our natures,
as if that utmost staggering that is death were not
due us,
as if transmigration into gods, angels, demons, or
giants were not our
birthright, or our predestined conclusions.

2-8-12

Unspeakable Immensities

Just short of Paradise we stand in our bands at
water's edge,
goal in sight, yet not attainable until death at best.
Rising above the clouds and mist over there, Mount
Olympus,
Sinai, vine-venerated Vesuvius, Elysium beyond,
lands of milk and honey
where we can rest, recline with trilobites and mice,
with all
those others, without/within, with our enemies
and our friends,
then venture out into the interior of an indefinite
continental
expanse, on roads to high adventure, where danger
waits, and deepest mystery.
Those who go far enough in are never heard from
again, but
may be encountered as golden forms among the
crags
and trees, haunting presences,
both benevolent and fierce, having incorporated all
opposites,
become more real thereby, and thinned unto
unspeakable immensities.

3-26-13

Certain Wondrous, Healing Kisses

Those who knew one another on earth most
intimately,
breath-by-breath and by caresses, fingertips
to nape of neck, palm to inner thigh, brimming
glint to
glint, tooth to lip, breast to spine, mind to
kindled spirit,

when one passes through that dash-and-dazzle,
shadowed
membrane or fog-enveloped portal to afterworlds,
beyond, behind, disapparates vis-à-vis this specific
venue,
existentiation of the blind,

re-acquires in dimensions of enchantment herself
once more,
gains in stature, increasing incrementally or by
the velocity of light, more fulsome knowledge,
wisdom,
wholeness, bliss,

becomes almost another being from that which she
had
formerly exhibited, projected or portrayed, or at
the very least is changed along pathways which
first become
accessible

in such illuminated and expansive landscapes or
domains,
burgeons, wings, or trudges toward some state
of being her of which her life on earth had
manifested
merely as
prefigurations;

when those, or that particular one she loved,
incarnate each —
glance to glance, lilt to scolding, rib to rib —
stands freshly past that threshold she herself
traversed, moments,
eons since, naked, trembling, swaying on
unsteady feet,

will she still know him, love him, recall those
intimacies
by which these two were bonded in that realm of
birthing, now vanquished, in which they played
their fetal scenes and aided
each the other
in unfoldment,
maturation, even flourishing,

one and other's growth of spirit and the soul, or
will she nod
peremptorily, turn away, or sit awhile with him,
lightly, barely grazing whatsoever may lie at hand,
explain in

the kindest words available why divorce, she from
he,

must be final, smile, flash away, be lost again in
light-filled
fastnesses or numinous clouds: *akhu*, saints, angels
or divinities?

What if angels, tall as trees, stretched out long and
fervent,
minus bones and flesh like ours, DNA or genitalia,
stride oceans, the hide of these some unspeakable
fluorescence,
burn cold as frosted glass, holiness in-place

of psyches as we know them, prodigious, coursing
hearts?
Whatever virtues such creatures may possess as
these, being human in some most authentic sense
is not listed in
their pedigrees.

If they do not marry, that loss is theirs.[128] The
human entity,
although resurrected, germinated seed of earthly
life raised up a new creation, human in its origin,
is human still, and ever,

---

[128] Reference to one of Jesus' teachings about angels and the
resurrected/transfigured dead: the New Testament, Gospel
of Luke 20:34-36

has that ancient primate stamp forever in its looks
and features —
as well, part-and-parcel, at its core in an aetheric or
pneumatic way.

God values human beings, seeks their ripening,
that which is
particular to them, and, although they flash,
thunder, billow, grow vast and bright of aspect,
has no interest
in their transubstantiation unto some wholly alien

species. When perfection is attained in their
peculiar mode,
they warm and warm, become more daunting,
whole, as demi-gods or demons.

Interior to every being en route to Deity is that
primordial form
with which it was instantiated. There is not one
kind in Heaven, but many species, all divinized
according to
their given natures — not all suns or moons, stars,

or spheres of harmony or of light — but diverse as
guinea pigs,
elephants, cats and fish — and apotheosis is gained
or granted as each individual, *as* individual and as
member
of those comprehensive

categories by which she or he is named, reaches its
epitome:

those *loci* in a ring, alongside every other, where
each tribe,
and those ipseities emerged from these, cross this
boundary of sublime irradiation, thereby enter
Heaven,
what Plotinus called "the Intelligible,"
and is completed precisely as he or she was
actually, and is, on
and on into Infinity.

Therefore, when that man sways trembling white
and stitchless
beneath some sun which never swells nor gutters,
and looks for her, lonely, hoping, with wind-blown
cloak, like silver and like gold,
she runs to him, or flies, alighting,

flings that robe she's woven for this occasion about
his shoulders,
with fullness of her countenance, unabated yet
distilled, meets him where he stands, with *her* love,
albeit greater, wise and deep —
still, recognizable
to him upon the instant —

and identical and not
to those he'd known on earth, embraces him,

fulfills his love for her, and hers for him, with certain wondrous, healing kisses.

8-31-09

The Dead Loom Ever Loftier

The dead, I think, loom ever loftier, identity upon
identity,
blooming from their tombs like rain-presaging
clouds

or stands of ancient trees, until their tops are lost in
light,
and quaffed and dissipated in exultant, chanting
crowds!

8-29-09

480

When I Am Winged

When I am winged beyond the grave,
I do not wish those of doves or eagles,

but rather dragonflies — that translucent
rainbowed cellophane, veined, and subtly
sheening.

I should like to dart, dance, dive, hover,
shoot out like a rocket, and alight at my
convenience.

I would certainly like the use of clouds for
sofas, but would prefer piling, purple
thunderheads to simple cotton
cumulus.

Though I like the sound of harps and lyres,
I'd rather manufacture lightning and
learn to play the *aulos*.[129]

And when I seek companionship, I think I'll
seek, not saints or angels, but those who
show a little darkness.

11-16-13

---

[129] Aulos: Ancient Greek double flutes

Lifting Spirit into Bliss

However Changed

However changed we may become once we've
turned away from this mirror's smoky glint,
I'm convinced we'll recognize each other and be
reunited by embraces and long-drawn kisses
in that wonderland that whelms behind us now,
but then will be our whole environment.
And the love we feel for each other here, and do
our best
to demonstrate, will there flow fully, without
interruption, impediment, or stint.

11-17-13

485

Into High-ness

Within some supra-celestial dusk that neither
yields to lightening nor abides a falling off forever
into night-ness;
upon some timeless dawn that neither ripens
toward ten o'clock or noon, nor darkens back to
moonlight;
at some summit of high translucence which neither
stiffens toward opacity nor dissipates in blinding
brightness,
we slant a ladder to this garden wall, ascend its
cantilevered thrust of rungs, poke our heads
through vines,
above limed whiteness,
and, gaze transfixed, pitch headlong, past facticity,
into that gravityless fantastic, sheer now, lifting
into High-ness.

1-31-15

The Upper Darkness

Above our glossy atmospheres, beyond those
astonishing arcs and icy cirruses of our light-speed
out-bound dreams,
where, breathless, vacuumed clean, the whirling
vortices subside in shadowed fathoms deeper than
that lifeless crypt of Jovian seas,
that's where Mystery delves, unblinking, parts the
void and whelms us in, when we no longer touch,
taste, smell, or see.
God, though He is Himself that Mystery, slays and
resurrects us by His Love in the upper darkness of
His Infinity.

10-9-15

There Is Fullness above Us

There is Fullness above us.
There is nothingness beneath us.
Who would not seek to ascend?

There is Light above us.
There is darkness beneath us.
Who toward that Light would not bend?

There is Love above us.
There is infinitely less than heedlessness
beneath us.
Who would not seek to love and be loved
without end?

8-5-13

Daedalus

Throughout that sweltering Minoan summer,
Daedalus,[130] the
careful craftsman, worked, with wax, stylus,
papyrus, glue and reeds,
drafting first what no human hand had ever traced
on paper.
In his tower beneath the double axe and bull horns,
he labored mightily above the sea.
Confined there as a captive in Knossos' sprawling
palace, he
gathered feathers from those doves which flickered
past his window, now and then
alighting.
Thus he worked, spine curved like a flexed bow,
painstakingly
contriving over floor and table some culminating
and transformative device
by means of which he dreamed of shedding
gravity's
enslavement, thrusting through his open window,
flinging himself upon the air, and flying.
So he labored, until one night, when breeze
flowed
velvet across the dolphined sea,

---

[130] Daedalus: In ancient Greek mythology, Daedalus and his
son Icarus escaped captivity on the island of Crete by making
wings of wax and feathers.

wax and glue hardened, cured, and dried,
Selene
bobbing like a fisherman's cork afloat upon the
rhythmic waves, then rose and
steadied, sidling up across the vaulted wastes of
heaven,
cried in silent majesty
her co-extensive wildness and tranquility, and
lured him to
the window, *mysterium tremendum*.[131]
Trembling, he fitted on his wings, climbed,
crouched,
his strapped and pinioned arms pressed close
against his body, swayed
a moment, nearly fainting, panicked by the height,
gazed down and
out into that silvery blackness, felt a certain
tracklessness
below, waiting to envelope him, then flexed his
thighs and feet,
pushed off, and plummeted like a stone or iron
ingot,
wrenched out his arms against the hurricane he
himself was making,
pulled hard against the feathered sheets,
bounded
upward, wings filling, soared steeply, caught the

---

[131] Mysterium tremendum: Latin for "Tremendous Mystery"

glint of moonlight, and found
that he was free!

1-30-08

Icarus

Icarus[132] was not wrong. He just had the wrong
equipment.
If he'd only resourced metaphor instead of the
literalistic,
he'd be flying still, with nothing to impede him.

11-3-13

---

[132] Icaus: While his father, Daedalus, made it across the
Mediterranean Sea safely, Icarus flew too close to the sun,
which melted the wax which held the feathers of his wings in-
place. The wings disintegrated, and Icarus fell to his death in
the Sea.

In All Our Occultations

In all our occultations we pass into the
metaphorical,
and find the world behind the world from which
all this arises mightily, shines, and unto that
suspires.

I tell you truly, that realm of fable is more massive
and compelling, yet may not be rendered literally,
nor definitively described.

1-11-15

Dawn

It dawns in bands of colored light inside.
There is nowhere else to go for dawn but in.
Imaginal lungs are filled. There is a first
breath drawn, a flood of dove-white light,
then cascading greens,
seen for the first time.

There has never been anywhere else to thrive.
There is nothing outside the mind — all the
creatures that we know, some we never have.
Fantastic!

Beyond, a gentle turbulence, a breeze which
chants through muffled thunderheads above
lush forest trees, prismatic stillness, utter quiet,
beyond cessation and beginning.
The world we knew is past.

There is no space outside the Psyche.
Imagination is the doorway to authentic life,
a place to which we rise with right, and find
ourselves at last,
awash in waves of unimpeding Light!

4-13-10

You Were Always Meant for Going

Don't become unglued at death. Don't leave
fragments of
remorse, anger, irresolution, or partial personalities
behind
to throng those tangled alleyways between this
world and
the next. If you come back, come back with your
mind
entire, as a full-blown person, flesh of some kind,
and soul.
Come down in light on a benevolent mission
to gift
familiarity to the grieving, to bring messages of
warning
or consolation to friends, advice about needful
transitions,
whether in the form of wavering apparitions or less
dramatically
in dreams. I don't want pieces of you, flotsam and
jetsam,
memory traces, unattached to you as you were,
transiently
compounding with the organism of a talented
medium.
If you're going to be an oracle, be that cleanly. I'm
not interested
in trivialities or gibberish. If you don't know where

you are
when you're not speaking, either because you're
not you, or
because that impersonating you're doing actually is
from
nowhere, then pull yourself together and go on. I
know there is
Light behind you. Turn around and walk toward it.
Don't be
afraid of losing your identity in That. Jesus said
there
are many destinations beyond it.[133] If there's a train,
board it.
Some beautiful personification of Deity will be
waiting for you
at the end of the line, wrap you in a cape of fire,
offer you
nectar and ambrosia. Then you shall be winged and
well-shod.
You were always meant for going. Now fly!

5-4-14

---

[133] A reference to one of Jesus' sayings in the New Testament,
the Gospel of John, chapter 14, verses 1-4

The Space beyond the Moon

There are shadows too deep to ford or swim
through,
and unless you're gifted with the art of walking on
viscous liquids or vapors,
perhaps it's best to take the long way round,
following the shore,
or, better still, hitch a ride on Pegasus or fly with
bright-eyed angels,
and that way reach that wished-for space
beyond the moon.

9-15-15

What Is Unfinished

What is unfinished here must have its completion
in some alternative dimension.
What is unlived on earth must be lived to its
fulfillment in some more fruitful
medium.
What remains unconscious of the total Self of each
of us is present as some world-abandoning
freedom.
What is mere potential in this world, elsewhere
must be rendered in climactic
forms of being.

What is stunted must be reconceived.
What is spoiled must be redeemed.
What is injured must be healed.
What is experienced as unjust must be
recompensed.
Blind alleys must be opened to vistas of loveliness
and undelimited extension.

However all this is accomplished, if God is Love,
there will be some sweep of iridescent wings,
doors flung back abruptly, some indescribable
shimmering unto Ultimacy of that essential
goodness of all that is, until that One from Which it
issued is recognized, reacquired, and we begin to
sing.

9-16-09

En-Heavening

I

Pelting up those fabled sea-blue roads on high,
invisible
to all but those who know them — this, with inward
visioning —
I race the frigid winds which whip the tops of
violet cumuli
to froth and spume, glittering crystals driving
wildly
through stratospheric
vastness, which rip the plumage from hawks and
sparrows,
and tumble these like ruined Icarus to earth. I hurl,
burning, to reach the seat of Deity —
He of veined and marbled mien, wide-muscled, of
golden
hair — conceive myself as welcomed, and as an
honored
guest in palaces of His imagining!

II

Winging through atmospheres of flaming mist at
dawn in
fabled gardens, where mingled roses, oaks, and
palms
gold and purple shadow-forms impress, neither
cellulose

nor ghostly, and birds of unknown origin utter
cries
and psalms,
I myself alight, cast sparkling raisin eyes upon the
site of my
new home, and spy that unaccustomed sun which
never
dims or dies.
So this is resurrection of the flesh, which I've put
by and
subsequently donned, some odd condition by
which
Christ is I, and He-and-I, and One!

III

Entire orchestras, and bands with cymbals, both
hidden and
displayed, arc in upon the psychic ear, some
species of
audible enlightening,
mirror-to-mirror wanging forth and back with
supra-celestial
force or fire, iterating multiplexity, incessant
dazzling
of the spirit,
out-cries from every re-imagined blade of grass,
fruiting tree,
herd, gaggle, podding, some unobstructed thrust of
joy

and wondrous bliss of leavening!
Where I had thought to take the place by storm, I find myself
en-heavening!

3-16-09

Where Love Is All There Is, and Sheer

If you find yourself deviating from the path of Love
like an errant moon or asteroid
shunted off its meant trajectory by gravity wells of
unplanned-for planets in the void,
and rushing toward, years or eons, some
eschatology,
a rendezvous of self-annihilating impact,
what will there be to do when the laws of
benighted
souls, like those of quantum physics,
click in as unalterable facts,
and the last that anyone will have heard of you was
a burning path of incandescent gasses?

I wish you harmony, exaltation, and the music of
the spheres. If that is not possible here,
then There, where everything follows its optimal
path, where Love is all there is, and sheer.

9-23-14

When I Lie Down at Last

When I lie down at last upon that golden bed from
which the drama of my departing will unfold,
costumes and masks set aside, strewn or neatly
packed in boxes to keep, toss, or to be sold,

I will gladly welcome back the guiding visions of
my youth—as well, all the knowledge of my senses
then:
tastes, touches, sights, sounds—the pageantry of
feelings, the exuberance of my mental strength.

I would like to enter Heaven then in a wash of light
that might remind me of a Maxfield Parrish sky,
and of sunlit summer afternoons, my wife and
daughter laughing in the hammock, or that time we
flew the kite.

Then I would relinquish all of that, without
forgetting, and climb to even greater heights.

11-5-13

Magic Mirror

Might I not get up then from my deathbed,
set myself before a magic mirror,
and as I gaze see something more of me than
I had previously revealed,
that which always lived within perhaps, obscured
by ego, bones, and skin, and, eyes
fixed upon the glass as if within a wondrous
dream,
raise gilded, wind-full wings,
spring up, ascend on unseen currents of the Spirit,
musty rushes skim,
alight in bright savannahs, learn quiet jubilation
there, touch and feel this — illimitable dominion?

1-28-06

Who Will Sing with Me?

Where is that pounded-out thunder of the sun, that
radiance at the Center of the God Who is One,

and where is the joy in the Deity of Love?

Where are the eyes to see these green hierophanies
in the leafing of trees, ears to hear cosmogony

in the heron's oracular lift and shriek?

Where are the opening hearts, where the minds
stupefied by lightning's strike?

Where are the souls shearing off into the Light?

Who will ride the clouds with me? Who will shout
out-loud with me? Who will sing with me

on the high roads to Divinity?

2-9-15

Resurrection

Resurrection is re-membering, deep calling to deep,
the latter answering from the haze of matter,

standing upright when the trumpet blasts full-
throated, and every nucleus is melted then or
shattered.

That cloud of atoms, one's most intimate
composition, one's near and necessary scaffolding,
collapses,

and this which was distilled from that—identity,
trailing alternative renditions of the same,

emerges from the cloud of birthing, or the cloud is
burned away what has now become extraneous or
hampering,

and one strides forth into a brand new Light, upon
a brand new Earth; above, a sky transfigured
utterly, blinding white and blazing!

11-23-10

Part Spirit and Part Earthen

None of us gets to Heaven uncontaminated.
We were in the world to get dirty,
and when we leave we'll be carrying armloads
of our animal deeds up to where
the Earth looks blurry.
I'm sure there was a purpose to our sojourn here,
although, for the life of me, I can't
with certainty discern it.
I do trust that God knows us well, and would
not impose on us unbearable burdens.
I believe He's fair, and that He fully expects us
to arrive part spirit and part earthen.

2-22-15

Beatified and Astounded

A thinning late morning drizzle, more diminishing
humidity
than curtaining cloud,
infinitizes, molecule by molecule, that high-flown
sheet of
aether awash with light and glazing,
as if the tranquil palaces of Deity had drifted
downward,
settled their exuberance upon sea and ground,
and filled
such space, which now has ceased to intervene,
with sun
enthroned, and softly brushed with glowing
fingertips
the glassy surface of that cerulean expanse, which
bodies
forth the deepest blues, and yet, horizoning,
upward
breathes, lifts like an insubstantial shroud,
and melts
into the whitening breeze. A single stone-pine
up-thrust
from rocky bed, of focus becomes indicative,
and I can see
a far-off promontory, across this misting reach,
descried,
though half-obscured by haze, pastelled in tannish

hues,
and trimmed in radiance, rising oracular, more
spiritual
than matter — from my vantage, vague, yet, over
there, not
mirage, but more than *terra firma*.
That's my Homeland, I am certain, and certainly I
will go there,
where an airy vision might remake my very form
and being,
where I might cry aloud with joy and gratitude,
and walk
among holy, wondrous things, hushed now in
silence,
beatified, and astounded.

1-21-13

No Me at All

When I glimpse the Mystery of that One, serene
and infinitely removed from every here-and-there,
cooler than boundary-less Arctic swells and heaves,
gauzy-luminous like a moon in falling-off-
forever night,
I see it filling all the room there is, erasing space
and the very concept of it, so that all that is, It is,
and will never come to an end, I tremble with
wonder and dread,
am fascinated unto wished-for vanishing, and I do
not desire to stand or sit or sing or taste or be at all
except as object of Its contemplation.
I swoon, then wish to run into It at the speed of
light, arms welcoming, no gain to me, no me at all
is left —
just That, the only Is there is, has been, or ever will
exist!

10-15-10

Inhabitant of Elysium

So, I ascend to that many-columned, shadowed
hall, twilit,
bird-haunted, smelling of cedar and humidity,
where Father El[134] with coiled beard and bovine
horns sits
upon his ivory throne and dreams His dream
or nightmare of reality,
and murmurs into ears of those who seek His
wisdom all
secrets but the last, which if He knows, He will
not speak it.
That may only be imparted if one goes higher,
above the realm
of Nature and its Dreamer, Who, of some
significance,
has permitted more than a little darkness to enter
into His
reverie, and marred the beauty of His thought
with cruelty and incompetence.

May He nonetheless be honored and blessed.

Above His palace stands another, white with
marble, gleaming,

---

[134] Father El: The ancient West Semitic High-God Who served
as a major ingredient in later conceptualizations of Yahweh,
the chief God of the Kennites and Judahites, subsequently of
the Jews

suffused with light, where smiling Zeus holds
court beneath diaphanous,
coffered ceilings.
I know He knows the secret. His right hand raised,
He points toward a dimension more expansive
where everything
that ever was or will be becomes itself completely,
stretches out to its own maximum of being,
and brightens to its unique ipseity.
I stand, eyes slitting up into that Void of Joy,
yearning to be free
of me, and infinite, yet also treasuring my identity,
unwilling to let that go, smear out, and render all
this richness
I have lived and been to indeterminate Deity,
into which I, and those and that I have loved,
would fully
become ourselves, yet stripped of existentiality.

So I dwell in Zeus' Heaven, and enjoy the company
of all those who
have not gone up, who do not desire Totality,
and have not yielded to that culminating wish for
dissipation and
transcendence.

I am happy to be myself, somewhere between
sparrow and the Spirit,
and consider my infinitized All-that-is-and-isn't
to be eminently in safe-keeping,

while I am that, and also this, for all eternity, if I will it—creature of
Nature, citizen of Heaven, and inhabitant of Elysium.

3-8-13

Paradise Is What You Dream It

It might be just this, Paradise — a wilderness of elk
ranging frozen tundra;
a poplar forest in a snowstorm; on an illimitable
sun-savaged plain, panting zebra;
or this: fabulous fabrics of the heart's smoothest
issuing, lighter-than-air tissues
fashioned by an uncanny presence, whispered out
with propitious ease,
a seamless garment for the soul to wear, with
nothing left of unfinished business —
everyone wishing every other exactly as they seem!

You move from one scene to another, additioning,
eventually enormously, encompassing more and
more, yet never reaching Everything,
until you're prepared to be it.

How shall I describe these multitudinous
dimensions, lingering, limitless,
spaces in the heart — above all, Love?
They're made of every millisecond of pleasure any
creature has ever known — grains of granite, silica,
powdered glass, joy, surprise, wonder!

O how glad, glad, glad with such a brimming
gladness have I here that I'll always smell the fresh
shavings
my grandfather planed from the wood for our new
stoop, our blue Formica table!

That I'll stride if I please with my wife and
daughter among the flowers of
Grant Park,
plunge chest-deep in waves of the August
lake's water!

I'll be that Greatfish of the myths, dividing at my
up-rising, feeding millions!

Now see those five fire mountains floating off the
Florida Keys, blue in this mist of mingling,

sky and sea, blooming pink and green, announcing
hurricanes, gusting visibly from within!

Paradise at first, I think, is what you dream it.

6-7-2000

Bliss into Infinity

Into Joy

You can, you know, walk straight into Joy,
like stepping from one room into another.
You'll have to leave your self behind to do it,
but you'll finally be free of all that clutter!

1-10-15

More Wondrous Even than Death or Life

When I, reverberate, have grazed the underside of
that
exalted All-thingness of every manifested thing,
discerned the Core comprising each circumference,
beheld
in utmost bafflement the forms and masks which
constitute the where's and when's of all there is or
may be,
run my fingertips across the strings of Love's
immaculate
immensity,
plucked one or more of these, throat-bolted from
the heart,
insistent upon singing, known beneath the
shamming
of my intellection, a realm whose depths may not
be sounded,
and experienced the Center of each instant,
I have found and touched such Joy, continuously
present by
means of intuition, sudden loftings, signs of
guidance
from inside
an illimitable pacific stillness, and discovered
myself within

a secret space more wondrous even than death or life!

9-5-05

Radiant and Unending Sleep

After numberless painted mansions, done mostly
in pastels,
gardens of fruits and flowers, dragonflies, bees,
shaded pools, nymphs, satyrs, earthly companions
re-rendered,
yet not made strange, extravagantly transfigured
beings,
forest paths that fall away in shrouded hollows,
sudden, sun-
washed glades,
palaces for full moons, quarters and their crescents,
Greek
temples, adventures, golden childhoods, stations of
bewilderment
and more encompassing intuitions — after we are
through
with these,
all epochs and eons, individuality at the same time
strengthened
and made vast beyond imagining, wide and bright
as summer seas,
we might stand at last before a magic doorway,
posts, limen, lintel
carved in hieroglyphs, yet signs that we can read —

an invitation to proceed, or not, from proximity to
the One Who's
dreamed this up to radiant and unending Sleep!

12-10-12

Poetry's Completion

There will be poetry until all that which it envisions
is actualized and experienced.
Then it will cease. In its place, Fullness will arise
like a fresh-struck sun, ejaculated
satisfaction, and rapturous completion.

5-13-15

Well-being

"What, then," he asked, "is the maximum of well-being?"
She replied, "When the end at last is joined to its beginning."
"That's it?"
"Well," said She, "that and all this gathered gleaming!"

11-7-15

Essay

Some Major Features of My World View

In the Foreword I alluded to certain core beliefs and an overall orientation in terms of my world view. Here, for those who might be interested, I'd like to say a little more. My hope is that this somewhat more ample account of my experiential (spiritual and intellectual) background, from which the illuminations flow, will contribute to the understanding, and where applicable, the helpfulness of them. I'm sure that a number of the beliefs which I've come to over the course of my life are clear from the illuminations. I want to emphasize that these are *my* beliefs. Nonetheless, I think many, perhaps most, maybe all of the pieces can be appropriated in one way or another by those readers/listeners who do not share these beliefs. At least I hope that's the case.

First of all, it's probably clear that central to my world view is my experience of faith in and love for a Deity Who, while Infinite and therefore unknowable in His/Her/Its Fullness by finite creatures like us), even so makes Himself/Herself /Itself immediately and infinitely available to us *as if* He/She/It were a Person. Because this Deity has infinite capacity, by definition, "as if" is absolutely and totally effective and real. Whatever else that Deity is, and in whatever guises He/She/It appears to us — necessarily "where we are at" at any given moment and in whatever state of consciousness and being—He/She/It is ultimately and encompassingly loving, and Love Itself.

Second, I believe in a fully and tangibly realized Life "after" life, or Life "above" life, which for me, in the end, amount to the same thing. Indeed, it has been my experience that we can participate to whatever limited degree in our own enormously more expansive states of consciousness and being—our eternal Selves or, in Christian terms, our "resurrection bodies"—here and now, before our biological deaths. I think there is a deep (or high) part of us that has never left Heaven.

At some point in the "Afterlife" we, as we have known ourselves on earth, will be fully re-integrated and re-united with these luminous Selves, whether incrementally or suddenly. Our optimum and ultimate condition, I suspect, is *apotheosis*—complete oneness with God. Along the way, both in this life and the next, we are *all* submitted to a process of "purification" (Judgment) and eventual reclamation, a process that involves both suffering and joy. I believe that process of purification and reclamation includes everyone and everything within, and *as*, the entirety of Creation.

Third, I've come to what for me is the working hypothesis that Nature—*all* of it—is alive, and animated by a Consciousness, an Intelligence, that in some way is "other than" that of the God of Love. At the very least, so it seems to me, what I would call "the Spirit of Nature" is a fragmentary realization of some aspect of the Deity — which is to say, not fully, or even adequately, representative of Him/Her/It. I have always loved Nature, and have been transported by Its breath-taking scope and beauty. At the same time, I have come to the conclusion that, while Nature is unspeakably beautiful, It is morally and ethically bankrupt. Its demonstrated indifference to the well-being of Its creatures is massive and evidently limitless — that is, except for Its interest in their capacities to reproduce with the kind of creative novelty that Nature seems to require for Its own Self-advancement in the direction of greater and greater Consciousness.

Viewed from this perspective, myths of the Fall, from many different religions and schools of philosophy, of Someone or Something from a position of absolute Fullness to equally absolute Emptiness, have come to make sense to me. The idea has struck me with great forcefulness that in Its cosmically evolutionary project, Nature resembles nothing so much as someone trying to wake up — say, from a coma following a catastrophic injury — perhaps after plunging from a great height. The Spirit of Nature, from my standpoint, is like an amnesiac struggling to recall and re-engage his or her former life—his or her former level of consciousness and being.

In the Western philosophical tradition, a similar idea was articulated by Plato. Plotinus, the third century C.E. initiator of what became known as Neoplatonism, taught that through a series of "irradiations" from the One—in effect, stages of a Fall from Perfection of Consciousness and Being to Unconsciousness—the Soul of Nature plummeted into Nothingness. Once It began to recover, It regretted Its separation from the One, the absolute Good, and has subsequently tried (through Its restless and desperate series of changes from one thing into another) to re-create the Fullness It once knew and was. But *on Its own terms* It cannot— ever—because It has lost Its Infinity, which also means Its absolute Wholeness. Nearly fourteen billion years after Its "Fall," It has managed to generate relatively intelligent creatures (like us, but almost certainly not limited to us) who, at least individually, can begin in moments of ecstatic consciousness to imagine that supra-time/space Realm that is our, and Nature's, Homeland.

Having said this, I also believe that the Fall of the Psyche into and *as* Nature was, and in Its attempt to re-create the All-thingness It lost though a succession of forms with evolutionary directionality, continues to be a catastrophe of great good fortune as well as horror, as the early Christian theologian Irenaeus claimed. The existentiation of all these wonderful and miraculous creatures is certainly an enrichment of the Divine that perhaps could not have happened otherwise. And, at least as far as creatures with even modestly developed consciousness are concerned, the experiential wealth gained through the journey, including the journey of re-ascension to the One, seems priceless and irreplaceable in an absolute or infinitely valuable and valued way. "In the end," so I believe, the Deity will save the Spirit or Psyche of Nature Itself, and "lift" It back into Its original, yet greatly enriched, state of Wholeness—what the Christian theologian Origen termed *apokatastasis panton*, the "salvation of all things."

Readers familiar with any number of philosophies and religious myths, both Western and Eastern, and including such schools as Middle- and Neo-platonism, Pythagoreanism, Stoicism, Gnosticism, and Hegelianism, among others, will recognize their influence on my thinking.

I realize of course that such a scenario, one which divides the Divine into levels of Self-alienation, does not solve the problem of theodicy. I haven't tried to solve this problem, but rather to accept what to me is the appearance of such a

Divine Self-alienation as *functionally* explanatory. I also realize that this all sounds rather mythological. It *is* mythological. But I believe it squares pretty well with the discoveries and insights of the modern sciences as well as with aspects of what has been termed "the perennial philosophy." Scientific world views, it seems clear to me, are also mythological in their underlying presuppositions. We live in a time when the myth of classical science, with its exclusion of a causally effective psyche and/or Psyche, is increasingly seen as an inadequate description of reality, and in which various proposals of "panpsychism" and "process," made by scientists themselves, are gaining traction in an on-going attempt to account for those aspects of our experience that classical science has previously ruled out of bounds, but which are necessary to make sense of the world in which we *actually* "live and move and have our being."

Fourth, it seems inescapable to me that we are only ever within Psyche. Everything we think, feel, learn, know, experience, and do occurs within, and even *as*, that medium. I agree that people, objects, events, and so on which we experience as if they were objective, or "outside" of our subjective identities, are what and "where" they seem to be, at least for practical purposes. But oddly perhaps, these objective experiences take place only "within" our specific subjectivities, which is to say, "within" our psyches. I can see no way around that. This means, for me, that my psyche is "where" everything comes to be, is, and passes out of existence. Psyche is "where" the universe (past, present, and future) *is*. Psyche is where God is. Once more, readers familiar with various Western and Eastern philosophical and theological traditions, including those mentioned above as well as Jungian depth psychology, will recognize these influences on my thinking about this issue.

Fifth, it has been my experience that thinking and feeling deeply along these and similar lines lead to an abiding sense of amazement, wonder, and awe; amazement, wonder, and awe lead to a durable sense of humility; and humility of this kind delivers us to authentic and, at least from time to time, encompassing Love, in Christian terms "agape."

These five main beliefs which ground and provide structure for my world view, with numerous permutations and nuances — all of this by necessity of my finitude provisional — are the major points about the pieces in this collection that I wanted to make. I don't want to turn what I wished to be a bit of further explanation of the beliefs embodied in the illuminations into a major theological and philosophical treatise, with all of the detailed and often convoluted arguments that such things require. Let me just say that the reader/listener may very well perceive additional beliefs, and in more fine-grained expression, within the illuminations. My hope is that the intellectual exploration of these lyrical testaments will be enjoyable. My main intention in writing and sharing the illuminations is, after all, not ideological but pastoral.

I would like to say a few words about how I arrived at these (and related) beliefs.

Since as early in my life as I can remember, I have experienced what have variously been called "altered states of consciousness," "spiritual experiences," and "parapsychological" events. Some of these appear in the illuminations. Many more do not. At the same time, these experiences, signs of a perhaps more than usually permeable boundary between my ego-consciousness and Whatever-Else-There-Is, rather thoroughly inform all aspects of my world view, even when not obvious or explicit.

Also at an early age, along with my mainline Protestant up-bringing, I came to experience the Divine in a multitude of forms, both Pagan and Judeo-Christian-Islamic-monotheistic. Among the most impactful Pagan God-images for me have been: Amun-Re, Isis, Osiris and other Egyptian gods and goddesses; Zeus, Athena, Persephone, Dionysus, and Hermes among those of ancient

Greek provenance; Jupiter Optimus Maximus and Sylvanus (Roman); Father El of the Canaanites; and Cernunos of the Celts. The extra-Pagan monotheistic God-images which have been powerfully influential for me include Yahweh-Elohim of the Hebrews, Allah of the Muslims—particularly as experienced through a series of Sufi lenses—the Father God of Jesus and the early Christians, and, informed by all of these, especially the latter, a Cosmic as well as a Supra-cosmic Consciousness. All of these God-images impress themselves upon me as *real* in a way that is undeniable for me. They are all "concretized" and effectual psychic realities with Which, or Whom, I am in relationship. At the same time, the dominant God-image, the one against which I evaluate and by which I integrate all the others, is unquestionably some version of a comingling of the "Father" of Jesus (the God of Love, which, from my standpoint, was lived extraordinarily through the life, death, and resurrection/transfiguration of Jesus) and the Cosmic and Supra-cosmic Consciousness models (the former of these perhaps understood as "the God of the physicists"). This inclusivistically monotheistic experience of Deity is the most awe-inspiring, the most life-enhancing, and the most soul-growing of all of my encounters with what I have interpreted as God.

I began my intellectual life wanting to be a cos-
mologist. That changed to wanting to be a paleontologist, then an Egyptologist, then a theologian-
philosopher (with a particular emphasis on the
field of comparative religion), and eventually a
depth psychologist. I've had the enormous pleasure
of exploring these and other fields in significant
depth. I've had the good fortune to live in many
universes of the mind and heart, and these have all
shaped, guided, and schooled my emotional and
intellectual identity. Vocationally, I became a pastor, a pastoral counselor, a teacher, and a writer.

To extend the ideological self-identification I
gave in the Foreword: when asked what my
theological orientation is, I have sometimes res-
ponded by saying, "I am an Egypto-Hellenic Neo-
platonic/Gnostic Christian Universalist." By this I
mean, among other things, that I have been crafted
experientially and intellectually within this particular stream of spiritual development, which I
experience (in a vaguely Hegelian way) as a co-
herent succession of ever-evolving and recursive
complexly interwoven traditions of feeling and
thinking one's way from the explicated world into
Elysium (Heaven, Paradise), which infuses, inter-
penetrates, transcends, enfolds, and redeems this
present more limited, glorious but myopic world. It
is this stream of spiritual development that has
enabled me, in anticipation of my completed "re-

surrection," to live my earthly life with deep and finally unutterable appreciation and to lift my spirit into the Bliss that I believe ultimately awaits us all.

If this book of lyrical illuminations encourages, aids, and augments your own journey through this wondrous, teeming world to that Other, then I would be very pleased indeed, and feel that I have after all served a good and fulfilling purpose in my life.

A Commentary on *At the Thresholds of Elysium: Lyrical Illuminations for Lifting Spirit into Bliss*

At the Thresholds of Elysium: Lyrical Illuminations for Lifting Spirit into Bliss from a Jungian, Post-Christian, Spiritually Democratic Perspective

By Steven Herrmann, Ph.D., MFT, Author of
Spiritual Democracy: The Wisdom of Early American Visionaries for the Journey Forward

Douglas Gillette's *At the Thresholds of Elysium* powerfully presents the careful and thoughtful record of many breakthrough moments that came together for the author in a series of lyrically inspired prose-like poems with subtle yet captivating cadences and schemes of rhyming. The bulk of these were written between the years 2000 and 2015 while he was functioning vocationally in four sacred roles as: 1) a pastor; 2) a pastoral counselor; 3) a teacher; and 4) a writer. These four callings are all expressed by one central Voice that flows seamlessly throughout this new book in a generous outpouring of Oneness of Spirit. Here Douglas gives us his own version of a new dispensation of Light, Goodness, Wholeness, and Love at the threshold of a New Age, one which some contemporary thinkers have termed the "Age of

Aquarius." For those with an appreciation of astrology, this means that the lyrics were all written during the relative time of exit of the Sun from the constellation of Pisces, at the very dawn of that Age. As such, they suggest a portentous heralding of something that may be just on the cusp or cross-over point of our collective awareness. From my perspective, this signifies the awakening of an image of human-Divine Wholeness, or our collective "divinization" as a species.

What might this new myth of "Aquarius" be in the pulsing and soothing forms of it which Gillette dispenses to us? What might his lyrical illuminations have to contribute to the evolution of this emerging myth in our present space and time? Is there some synchronicity involved in the book's publication date of 2016? After all, 2016 is a multiple of four — historically for mystics as well as scientists, a central embodiment of the notion of human-Divine Integration. Notwithstanding evidence to the contrary, is there a movement afoot that might be called trans-religious or even trans-ideological, one which could carry us beyond a whole variety of previous dispensations, including those of the three major Western monotheisms, the Scientific Revolution, the Enlightenment, modernity, and even post-modernity? C.G. Jung as well as many other researchers, "prophets," and "seers" have certainly thought so. The experience of such a trans-religious and trans-ideological stance would require the evolution of human awareness in the direction of a non-parochial and comprehensive Super-consciousness.

Clearly, something Divine, wonderful, holy, and meta-scientific is speaking through Gillette's poems! As I am suggesting, this "something" proclaims a new myth that sounds a profoundly ecumenical note, one which announces the advent of a coming spiritual and ideological syncretism, a mutual fertilizing of world views, and a culmination of trans-religious and trans-ideological movements. Such a culmination under the guidance of Super-consciousness, in which oneness and multiplicity would thrive together, I have termed "Spiritual Democracy." The well-known Jesuit priest, paleontologist, and theologian Teilhard de Chardin (who famously coined the term "Cosmic Christ" in order to conceptualize, and in a sense begin to actualize, the mutual fructification that spirituality and science might yet realize) had a momentous, sky-wide vision of Christ in the desert of China while he was excavating Peking Man in 1916. This vision transfigured him utterly, and led him to develop a new *mythos* of a universalistic Christianity, one which would embrace all ideologies within an overarching Christian framework. Gillette goes further than Chardin, however, in his expression of a world-encompassing vision of the human spirit en route to eventual oneness with the Divine.

Gillette writes simultaneously as a depth psychological theorist and as a pastor. He writes from a standpoint situated in his personal belief in a resurrected, resurrecting, and ultimately illimitable Consciousness. He give us this version of a universalizing Christian—in this sense, perhaps, "post-Christian" (and post-Judaic, post-Islamic, post-modern, post post-modern)—Voice that intends, throughout his lyrics, to elevate the consciousness of the reader-listener of all faiths as well as agnostic and even atheistic persuasions, and thereby transform our awareness into an extraordinary state of mind, conscious of its subjective identity with pure Spirit. This alone, not to mention the beauty and power of the language of this Voice, makes *At the Thresholds of Elysium* uniquely and compellingly experiential. Gillette gives us practical examples of experiences of pure Light and Bliss through his descriptions of the soul-transforming spiritual insights and vistas of sages, mystics, and saints from many different cultures— Egyptians, Greeks, Christians, Sufi's, for example— that all correlate around a Center of Love. Gillette writes from his perspective within a largely, yet not exclusively, Near Eastern-Western venue. As a Westerner, I feel a deep sense of gratitude that these scintillating lyrics, whatever alternative spiritualities they may also encompass, are so finely attuned to the three primary monotheisms that have emerged from this wide-ranging geography and from the extraordinarily creative peoples which have inhabited it.

Douglas' regard for the reality of what Jung called the "objective psyche" shines through clearly in such poetic statements as "…it seems inescapable to me that we are only ever within Psyche." What Gillette has done in this beautiful book is to provide a close record of an integration of his discursive knowledge in the fields of comparative religion, world mythology, theology, philosophy, depth psychology, and the sciences through what again I would call the "post-Christian" lens of a spiritually enlightened theologian and counselor who is Self-aware. This means for Gillette that Psyche is finally where God is and God is where Psyche is, and Cosmos and Psyche are therefore one. While the astute reader will recognize that Jungian depth psychology has had a profound influence on Douglas' thinking about the Divine, his "illuminations" seem to take us beyond the "fourth" incarnated principle of Order—i.e., Jung's theory of individuation—and toward a distinctly *metaphysical* Self-realization, whereas Jung, constrained by a scientific world view, tended to leave an explicit metaphysics aside. We see this, for instance, in the lyric "Paul and His Mirror," where Douglas writes:

There is no space outside the Psyche.
Imagination is the doorway to authentic life,
a place to which we rise with right, and find
ourselves at last,
awash in waves of unimpeding Light!

Is this poem a description of an "imagined" reality alone, or is it a proclamation of an empirically experienced Reality which includes causality, space, and time, and is incarnated in mind and matter through the miracle of Gillette's reflective consciousness within a cosmos of infinite extension that is also inclusive of Jung's principle of synchronicity, which completes this "holy trinity" of physics? Has Douglas perceived and broken through to something in the space-time continuum in which a-causal connections have been taking place through meaningful coincidences, correlations (again, Jung's "synchronicities") across the world's ideologies? Through some kind of foreknowledge — that is, in the collective unconscious — has Douglas been enabled to tap into an Absolute Knowledge, albeit mediated by his role as pastor? The accent Douglas places on

Light, Love, and the Deity as both "Supra-cosmic Consciousness" and intimate Companion appears to be outside the range of concerns of most depth psychologists, and squarely within the domain of metaphysics.

Gillette's hope is that the intellectual exploration of his lyrical testaments will be enjoyable for the reader, but this hope, I feel, is his humility speaking; for his central aim is not simply enjoyment in the little "e" sense, but Enjoyment in a large capital "E" and transpersonal and supra-sensual Sense. His intention in writing and sharing his illuminations is not ideological, for as he rightly says, they are primarily *pastoral*. That is his true vocation speaking. I will add that by "pastoral" they are meant not only to guide the perplexed of the Christian "flock" (although that is part of what he is offering), but rather, thankfully, to initiate us all at the threshold of a new "testament" which is elevating, revealing, and verifying of an emerging Truth that goes beyond any institutionalized ideology, and affirms that we are all deeply one. He does not call the Supra-cosmic Consciousness he cites "Christ Consciousness" *per se* (although It is not *not* that), because he seeks to convey a more inclusive term.

Douglas has felt his way ever so carefully from the Christian notion of the explicated "Word of the

Father" to his own lyrical illuminations of Elysium (Heaven/Paradise), and thereby into an earthly anticipation of his, and our, completed "resurrections." Indeed, the ultimate aim of Douglas' lyrics is to lift his spirit and ours up into the Bliss which he believes ultimately awaits us all—not after our deaths alone, but in this very materialized existence. The marriage of mind and matter is what is at stake here. That marriage completed, Douglas urges us to finally embrace their culminating separation. As he says, there must be relative stability in our this-worldly configurations in order for us to optimally enter Elysium within the eternal Now. Gillette writes:

Also—the real point—because only when there's
relative stability in the lower dimensions of
psyche
can the spirit,
which is the best of us, be freed to climb into
the Light,
the Homeland of our most authentic biding.

These are not the intellectual musings of a rationalistic theologian, but the transformed, and transformational, lyrics of a man with many religious experiences of, as the Lutheran theologian Paul

Tillich put it, the "God beyond God," and earlier, as Meister Eckhart urged, a process of "leaving God for God." Douglas invites us each as readers-listeners to join our eternal Selves, essences, or, in Christian terms, our "resurrection bodies," to the myth of eternal Light and Cosmic Bliss here and now, before our biological deaths.

He makes his belief experientally valid and translucent in his poem "The Transformation of Aquinas" (the famous author of the *Summa* who had a spiritual encounter that made him feel that everything he had written hitherto was straw), where Douglas, speaking from his own altered state of consciousness, says specifically, "I myself have seen in moments of lofty pause and exaltation—/in the presence of which every thing is shown to be precisely what it is—/and all, light and shadow, lacking error, without flaw, unspeakable Goodness—/beauteous, wondrous, true, with such thrill/the soul experiences unexpected confirmation, and the rolling heart ceases its careening." While Aquinas put down his pen after his encounter with unsurpassable Light, Gillette has kept on writing! So too in, "There It Is!" Douglas declares his objective experiences of "resurrection":

I myself, awake three nights and
days, beheld a golden disk, eight feet in
diameter, set on
edge, just beyond my kitchen, upright on
the floor...
a computer of sorts — chips, circuitry, codes,
rivulating toward the center — all trajectories
of thought, dimensions without number,
love, death, resurrection, fashioned with
solidity, yet imaginal, right there,
past the cutting board!

There's the number four again (4 X2 = 8; vertical
and horizontal axes = 16, as in 2016)! This time the
"Akashic records" of Douglas Gillette are being
preserved in "a computer of sorts" — in a modern
image of a technological mandala, thereby dis-
playing the comfortable way he has of experiencing
as non-contradictory the truths of both science and
spirituality. I would say that "salvation" for Gillette
consists of recalling such moments of transcendent
experiences in the midst of our earthly lives, and
through the responsible recalling of these, learning
to move lyrically with the poet-pastor beyond the
daily life level of consciousness, toward higher and
brighter expressions of the Supra-cosmic Self — and
in that way "lifting spirit into Bliss."

All I can express finally is my heart-felt thanks to Douglas for having written this splendid volume!

Steven Herrmann

June 25, 2016

Made in the USA
Lexington, KY
04 November 2016